Come Write With Me:

POETRY

Workbook & Journal

Brooke E. Wayne

For CHILDREN Volume 1

Hearts & Flowers
Publishing

Additional Poetry Activities at www.brookeewayne.com under "POET'S CORNER" are free to use in the classroom for instructional purposes.

Chief Editor: Anette Blaskovich

Title: Come Write with Me: POETRY Workbook & Journal (For Children)
Author: Brooke E. Wayne
Publisher: Hearts & Flowers Publishing
Excerpts: Public Domain
Cover Photo: Shuttershock
Font: American Typewriter, Zuka Doodle, Gallaghar
Graphics: Pixabay.com, PublicDomainVectors.com, Vecteezy.com membership
ISBN: 9781734163728
IMPRINT: 1734163728

Description: This is a workbook loaded with creative writing tools to compose poetry that includes fill-ins, worksheets, examples, structured writing exercises, categorical word lists, creative writing prompts, and much more!

Category: Creative Writing Workbook, Creative Writing Journal, Poetry Workbook, Poetry Journal, Creative Writing Prompts, Poetry Writing Prompts, Poetry Starters, Creative Writing Starters, Standards-based Poetry Lessons, Creative Writing Lessons, Structured Creative Writing, Instructional Workbook, Poetry Curriculum, Poetry Lessons, Elementary School Poetry, CCSS Aligned Curriculum, Homeschool ELA Workbook

A Special Thank You to Anette Blaskovich for your brilliant editing skills and insight into the elementary mind.

And thank you Robin Woods for your final editing and visual expertise.

TABLE OF CONTENTS

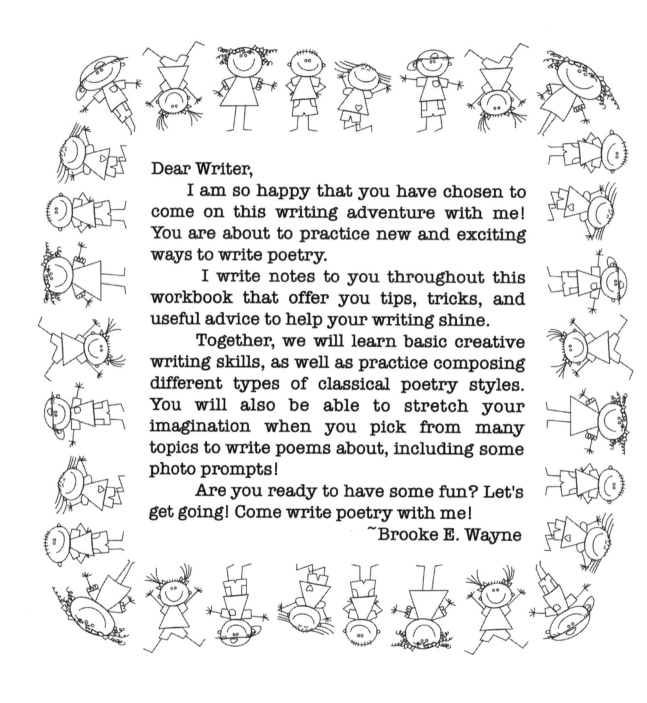

Dear Writer,

I am so happy that you have chosen to come on this writing adventure with me! You are about to practice new and exciting ways to write poetry.

I write notes to you throughout this workbook that offer you tips, tricks, and useful advice to help your writing shine.

Together, we will learn basic creative writing skills, as well as practice composing different types of classical poetry styles. You will also be able to stretch your imagination when you pick from many topics to write poems about, including some photo prompts!

Are you ready to have some fun? Let's get going! Come write poetry with me!

~Brooke E. Wayne

HOW TO USE THIS BOOK

Every poet is a unique person
unlike anyone else
the same way every poem
has its own special personality.
My hope is to help you become a better writer
through the tasks I have created for
Come Write with Me:
POETRY
Workbook & Journal
(For Children)
Once you complete the tasks in the beginning,
you can keep going in order,
or you can skip around in this workbook.
It's up to you!
I will be with you the entire journey
cheering you on,
giving you advice and tips,
and helping you be
the best writer you can be.
I also have a surprise for you.
This workbook has lots of graphics in it
for you to color, too!

LITERARY TERMS

POETIC DEVICES: Figurative language used to enhance a poem

FIGURATIVE LANGUAGE: Expressions not meant to be taken literally that enhance the understanding of different writings in a creative way

STANZA: A group of lines in a poem--the way essays are made up of paragraphs, poems are made up of stanzas, and stanzas are made up of lines (also called verses)

VERSE: A line of poetry

END RHYME: The ends of two or more lines of poetry that rhyme together

FREE VERSE: A poem that cannot rhyme

POINT-OF-VIEW (POV): The perspective in which writing is told from

First Person POV Pronouns: I, My, Me, Our, We, Us, Myself, Ourself, Ourselves

Second Person POV Pronouns: You, Your, Yours

Third Person POV Pronouns: He, She, Him, Her, They, Their, Theirs, Them, His, Hers, It, One

RHYME SCHEME: Alphabetically labeling the ends of lines of poetry that rhyme together, creating a pattern (Example: ABAB, CDCD, EFEF)

Extended Example:
> I wanted to play in the <u>sun</u> (A)
> And have my friends join <u>me</u> (B)
> So we could all have some <u>fun</u> (A)
> Enjoying each other's <u>company</u> (B)

(SUN and FUN rhyme together, so they are assigned A, the first letter of the alphabet. ME and COMPANY rhyme together, so they are assigned B, the next letter in the alphabet.)

SYLLABLES: Parts that create a word, broken up by beats or pauses
Examples: car (1 syllable) wa-ter (2 syllables) happ-i-ness (3 syllables)

Creative Writing
Toolbox

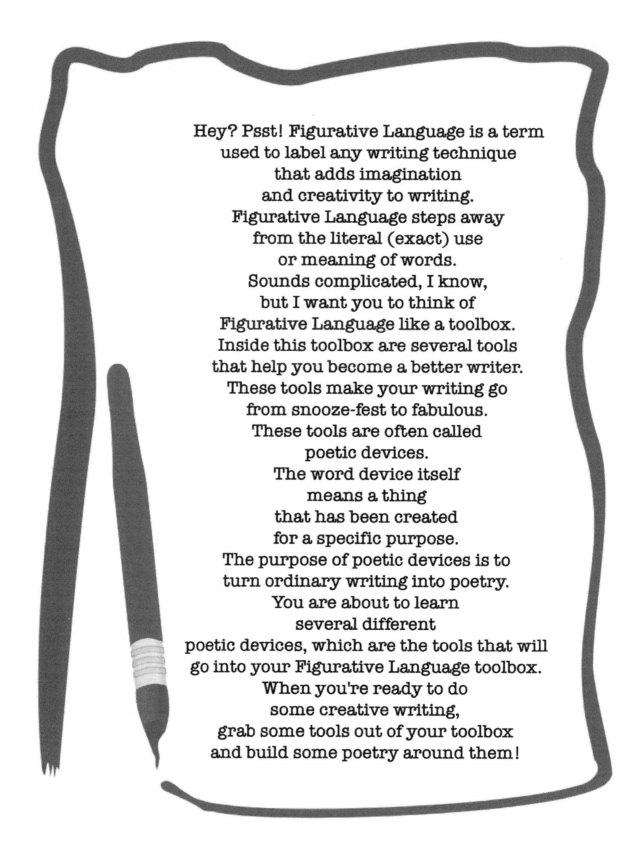

Hey? Psst! Figurative Language is a term
used to label any writing technique
that adds imagination
and creativity to writing.
Figurative Language steps away
from the literal (exact) use
or meaning of words.
Sounds complicated, I know,
but I want you to think of
Figurative Language like a toolbox.
Inside this toolbox are several tools
that help you become a better writer.
These tools make your writing go
from snooze-fest to fabulous.
These tools are often called
poetic devices.
The word device itself
means a thing
that has been created
for a specific purpose.
The purpose of poetic devices is to
turn ordinary writing into poetry.
You are about to learn
several different
poetic devices, which are the tools that will
go into your Figurative Language toolbox.
When you're ready to do
some creative writing,
grab some tools out of your toolbox
and build some poetry around them!

SIMILE

comparing two items together
that are not alike
using 'like' or 'as' between them

Dear Writer,
    A SIMILE is a poetic device that takes two items that have nothing to do with each other and helps show that they have something similar about them. This tool gives readers a better idea of what they are imagining when they read your poem. I can't wait for you to practice writing some verses using similes.
Come Write With Me,
Brooke E. Wayne

EXAMPLES

The fall **clouds** are **as fluffy as cotton candy.**
My hungry **stomach** growled **like** a snarling **bear.**
Mary is as busy **as** a **bumblebee** in springtime.

Brainstorm

Emotional Similes

love like/as a warm blanket
angry like/as a raging storm
hurt like/as a stubbed little toe
peaceful like/as a sleeping baby
happy like/as a kid in a candy store
sad like/as a dog in an animal shelter
scared like/as a fish caught on a line

Action Verb Similes
(Action Verbs show physical movement)

laugh like/as a hyena
shout like/as a trumpet in my ear
whisper like/as a floating feather
giggle like/as a baby playing peek-a-boo
scream like/as air being let out of a balloon
growl like/as thunder rolling over the mountain top

_____

_____

_____

_____

_____

_____

_____

_____

_____

_____

_____

_____

_____

_____

_____

_____

_____

_____

METAPHOR

A direct comparison
of two items that are not alike
(does NOT use 'like' or 'as')

Dear Writer,

    A METAPHOR is a lot like a simile. Both of these poetic devices take two items and compare them together so that they somehow have similarities. The difference with this tool is that the two items are compared as if one is the other. Words like 'is' or 'was' are used instead of 'like' or 'as'. You know they are not the same thing, but you get to imagine that they are poetically. Metaphors can also be implied or stated in a way that makes you have to guess what the other item is based on what it is doing.

Come Write With Me,
Brooke E. Wayne

EXAMPLES

The white **kitten was** a **snowball** of fur.
The **girl is** a **mermaid** swimming all summer long.
The **memory flooded** my mind. (implied metaphor: water)

Brainstorm

Metaphors

time is/was a thief
happiness is/was a dance
friendships are/were a garden
children are/were her sunshine
little brother is/was a class clown
newborn kitten is/was a fluffy cotton ball
stars are/were pin pricks in a black velvet sky

Implied Metaphors
(Implied--compared indirectly, not using 'is')

cries an ocean of bitter tears
soars through the quiz with ease
breaking his heart to hear the news
coach barking instructions at the team
summer tastes of sweet sunshine and happiness
sunset splashing watercolored ribbons across the sky

_____

_____

_____

_____

_____

_____

_____

_____

_____

_____

_____

_____

_____

_____

_____

_____

_____

_____

_____

_____

_____

ONOMATOPOEIA

A written word that makes
the sound that word is describing
when it is said out loud

Dear Writer,

An ONOMATOPOEIA is a simple device with a fancy name. The purpose of this tool is to create sound effects. Think about 'whoosh'. Now, say it out loud. Notice that you just made the whooshing sound when you spoke it? Are you still trying to figure out how to pronounce this tool? You say it like this: ON-oh-MAW-toh-PEA-uh.

Come Write With Me,
Brooke E. Wayne

EXAMPLES

The water balloon landed with a **splat**.
She slammed the **squeaky** door with a **bang**.
He **gulped** the soda down so fast it made him **burp**.

Brainstorm

Onomatopoeia

argh, gah, whoosh
purr, boing, plop
hum, pop, zoom
bang, kerplunk, zoink
swish, splat, chatter
hiss, whirl, snarl
gurgle, squish, groan
howl, moan, squawk
crinkle, crispy, snap
growl, hush, squeal,
whisper, gulp, hiccup

The **howling** wind **whirled** around me
as my teeth **chattered** from the chill.
Then, suddenly, the **whooshing** wind halted,
and everything went still.

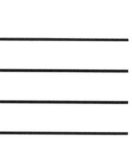

_____

_____

_____

_____

_____

_____

_____

_____

_____

_____

_____

_____

_____

_____

_____

_____

_____

_____

_____

_____

_____

_____

_____

HYPERBOLE

An extreme exaggeration
meant to make a point
but not meant to be taken literally

Dear Writer,

A HYPERBOLE is a poetic device that uses exaggeration to make a point in a dramatic or funny way. A hyperbole is not meant to be taken seriously because it would probably be impossible to be realistic. It's the world's greatest, most fantastic tool in creative writing! Just kidding. See what I did there will all the hyperbolic descriptions?

Come Write With Me,
Brooke E. Wayne

EXAMPLES

I'm so hungry **I could eat everything on the menu**!
The mom told her son **a million times** to clean his room!
He was so tired he said he could **sleep forever.**

Hyperbole

BIG: ginormous, massive, huge, tremendous, grand
SMALL: tiny, minuscule, itty-bitty, little, slight, petite
HOT: scorching, smoldering, boiling, roasting, scalding
COLD: chilling, freezing, icy, glacial, numbing, polar
HAPPY: joyous, ecstatic, heartened, golden, thrilled
SAD: blue, brokenhearted, forlorn, gloomy, sorrowful

Guess what?
When this poetic device is used with 'as',
it also doubles as a simile, too!

as quiet as snowfall
as fast as a speeding train
as angry as a raging storm
as sweet as a bag of jellybeans
as exciting as a three-ring circus
as crazy as a wild bull on the loose

_____

_____

_____

_____

_____

_____

_____

_____

_____

_____

_____

_____

_____

_____

_____

_____

_____

PERSONIFICATION

A non-human behaves like a human
or has humanlike characteristics

Dear Writer,

The poetic device PERSONIFICATION takes an item that isn't a human being and makes it do things a human could. It makes the item come to life by giving it emotions or physical movements that a human might feel or do. This tool brings excitement to your poems!

Come Write With Me,
Brooke E. Wayne

EXAMPLES

The **petals danced on the daisy** as the wind blew.
The **table legs** were made of wood.
The rocket **screamed** as it blasted across the sky.

Brainstorm

Personification

The leaves danced on the tree.
My scarf tried to strangle me.
Happiness squeezed my heart.
My journal hides all my secrets.
A rainbow arched its aching back.
Hope smiled down on her dreams.
The stars huddled together in the sky.
Sunshine wrapped its rays around me.
The ocean is calling me to go for a swim.
The candle flame licked at the darkness.
An angry cloud dumped rain on my head.
A blaring car horn shouted into the night.
My stomach growled in anger wanting to be fed.
The joyful flowers tilted their faces towards the sun.
Memories flooded my mind when I listened to that song.

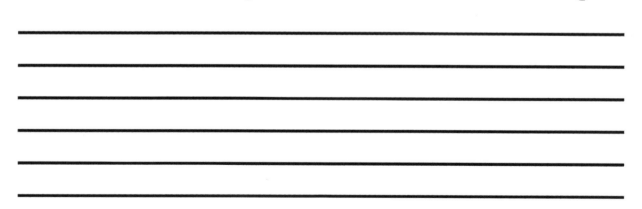

_____

_____

_____

_____

_____

_____

_____

_____

_____

_____

_____

_____

_____

_____

_____

_____

_____

_____

_____

_____

_____

_____

_____

_____

_____

_____

_____

_____

_____

_____

_____

_____

_____

_____

_____

_____

_____

_____

REPETITION

Repeating a word, phrase, line,
stanza, or idea in a poem

Dear Writer,

REPETITION is when you repeat something in your poem. It can be as simple as a word or as complicated as a whole stanza (which is what we call a paragraph in a poem.) Songs have repeated stanzas that are called choruses. You can even repeat similar words, and it still counts! This tool is wonderful because it helps the reader understand something by letting it sink in through repetition.

Come Write With Me,
Brooke E. Wayne

EXAMPLES

Round, and round, and round the merry-go-round goes.
Merrily, merrily, merrily life is but a dream.
The **lovely, beautiful, pretty** flower blossomed.

Repetition
(Similar Words)

Joyful: happy, pleased, content, jubilant
Excited: hyper, overactive, jumpy, antsy
Disgusting: awful, unpleasant, gross, revolting
Nice: polite, kind, friendly, pleasant, welcoming

Repetition
(Phrases and Lines)
(Repeat one of these phrases or lines several times in a poem.)

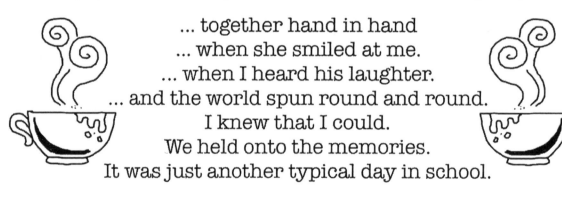

... together hand in hand
... when she smiled at me.
... when I heard his laughter.
... and the world spun round and round.
I knew that I could.
We held onto the memories.
It was just another typical day in school.

_____

_____

_____

_____

_____

_____

_____

_____

_____

_____

_____

_____

_____

_____

_____

_____

_____

_____

_____

_____

_____

_____

_____

ALLITERATION

Two or more words start with
the same letter and sound.

Dear Writer,
    ALLITERATION is that one poetic device you
probably already know but wasn't sure what it was
called. Have you ever heard of tongue twisters? Yep,
those words that all start out the same way are using
alliteration! This tool makes poetry sound spectacular!
                                            Come Write With Me,
                                            Brooke E. Wayne

EXAMPLES

The **t**icking clock **t**ells **t**ime perfectly.
She **s**aw the **s**unshine **s**parkling behind the clouds.
I **w**andered around **w**aiting for **W**aldo to show up.

Brainstorm

Alliteration as Tongue Twisters

Tacky **t**affy **t**ugged on my **t**ooth.
Carrie **c**reated a **c**andy-filled **c**upcake.
How long **h**ave you **h**ad those **h**ilarious **h**iccups?
A **p**retty **p**rincess **p**ranced around in **p**ink **p**ants.
A **b**ig, **b**lue **b**utterfly **b**uzzed around **B**etty and **B**rett.

Alliteration
(Phrases)

misty **m**orning
hopelessly **h**appy
green **g**rass **g**rowing
laughing **l**ike a **l**unatic
whimsically **w**ondering
pickles making me **p**ucker
bright, **b**eautiful, **b**lue skies

_____

_____

_____

_____

_____

_____

_____

_____

_____

_____

_____

_____

_____

_____

_____

_____

_____

_____

_____

_____

_____

_____

_____

_____

IMAGERY

The use of any of the five senses:
sight, sound, smell, taste, and touch

Dear Writer,

    IMAGERY is a poetic device that makes use of one's imagination. Can you see it in your mind? What if it smells? Does it make a noise? What does it feel like to the touch? If you could eat it, what would it taste like? You don't have to put all five senses in a poem for imagery to count, though. Remember onomatopoeia words? Any of those words count for sound imagery, and any color counts for sight imagery!

Come Write With Me,
Brooke E. Wayne

EXAMPLES

Sticky, sweet, chocolate ice cream dribbled down the cone.
The **juicy** cheeseburger **crisp** lettuce on it.
The **blue** bird **chirped** at my window.

Brainstorm

Imagery

SIGHT: colors, sizes
SMELL: scents, aromas
TOUCH: textures, sensations
TASTE: flavors, things you can eat
SOUND: onomatopoeias, sound effects

Imagery in Use

juicy peach
slippery ice
hot pavement
crunchy chips
musty gym bag
sweet strawberry
yellow school bus
humongous truck

A full list of Imagery Words and Colors are on pages 45-48.

_____

_____

_____

_____

_____

_____

The Sensuous World

Hey? Psst! When we think of poetry,
we often think of sing-songy rhyming lines.
We have already learned that
when you add poetic devices
to your creative writing,
you begin to build a poem.
Write down your feelings about something
or write a vivid scene
that someone can imagine clearly
in their minds then add some tools to it.
When you break up the lines
like I do with blurbs like this one,
it adds to the quality of creating a poem.
This next section focuses on Imagery.
The five senses are
sight, sound, smell, taste, and touch.
Collectively, they are considered sensuous,
meaning they each tap into one's senses.
Many of the poems ahead
are fill-in-the-blank in style.
If you want to change anything
about the formatted poems, do it.
Don't let the format stop you
from making each poem uniquely yours.
Look around you, listen carefully,
take a deep breath, enjoy each bite or drink
you consume, and recognize how
things feel physically in the moment,
and write down your experiences
to add to a poem some day.
For now, let's see what kinds of poems
you'll come up with that use lots of Imagery!

IMAGERY

SIGHT SOUND TASTE TOUCH SCENT

SIGHT	SOUND	TASTE	TOUCH	SCENT
All Colors	Onomatopoeias	Acidic	Abrasive	Aromatic
All Sizes	Barking	Acrid	Bristly	Briny
Bold	Breathy	Bitter	Bumpy	Burnt
Bright	Buzzing	Bittersweet	Clammy	Citrusy
Brilliant	Clanking	Bland	Cold	Dank
Cluttered	Clomping	Buttery	Creamy	Dusty
Curled	Croaky	Chalky	Doughy	Earthy
Curved	Crispy	Chocolaty	Fluffy	Fishy
Dark	Crunchy	Fresh	Furry	Floral
Dim	Dripped	Fruity	Humid	Foul
Dingy	Gong	Honeyed	Greasy	Fragrant
Dull	Groan	Lemony	Grimy	Full-bodied
Faded	Gurgle	Metallic	Gritty	Gamy
Foggy	Gutteral	Minty	Hairy	Garlicky
Glittery	Hoarse	Nutty	Hot	Herbal
Gloomy	Hiss	Raw	Icy	Malted
Glossy	Huff	Resfreshing	Jellied	Metallic
Hazy	Husky	Rich	Leathery	Moldy
Illuminating	Moan	Ripe	Liquid	Musty
Illustrious	Murmur	Roasted	Mushy	Peppery
Iridescent	Peep	Robust	Oily	Perfumed
Milky	Purring	Rotten	Powdery	Piney
Misty	Ringing	Salty	Prickly	Pungent
Murky	Rustle	Savory	Rough	Putrid
Pale	Shrilled	Smoked	Sandy	Rancid
Shabby	Sizzle	Soupy	Satiny	Rank
Shimmering	Slur	Sour	Scalding	Rotten
Shiny	Snivel	Spicy	Silky	Salty
Smudged	Strangled	Stale	Slick	Seasoned
Sparkling	Swoosh	Succulent	Soft	Smoky
Spotted	Thud	Sugary	Stiff	Spiced
Speckled	Thump	Sweet	Smooth	Spoiled
Straight	Tinkle	Syrupy	Sticky	Sulfuric
Wizened	Trickle	Tangy	Sultry	Stinky

RED ORANGE YELLOW GREEN

Baby Pink	Amber	Almond	Army
Berry	Apricot	Banana	Avocado
Brick	Auburn	Biscotti	Crocodile
Bubblegum	Cantaloupe	Blond	Emerald
Burgundy	Carrot	Brass	Evergreen
Carnation	Cheddar	Buttercup	Forest
Cayenne	Cider	Buttermilk	Grass
Cherry	Cinnabar	Butternut	Grasshopper
Chili	Copper	Butterscotch	Honeydew
Cinnamon	Coral	Canary	Hunter
Cotton Candy	Creamsicle	Candlelight	Jade
Cranberry	Fire	Cheesecake	Juniper
Crimson	Fox	Corn	Kelly
Currant	Ginger	Cream	Khaki
Fire Engine	Lava	Curry	Kiwi
Flamingo	Mango	Custard	Leaf
Fuchsia	Marigold	Daisy	Lime
Hot Pink	Marmalade	Dandelion	Mint
Lipstick	Melon	Dijon	Moss
Magenta	Papaya	Gold	Olive
Maroon	Peach	Goldenrod	Pea
Mauve	Persimmon	Honey	Peridot
Paprika	Pumpkin	Lemon	Pine
Pomegranate	Rust	Mustard	Pistachio
Punch	Saffron	Pear	Sage
Raspberry	Salmon	Pearl	Sea Glass
Rose	Sienna	Pineapple	Seaweed
Rouge	Squash	Sunflower	Spruce
Ruby	Sulfur	Straw	Green Tea
Scarlet	Sunset	Tan	Teal
Strawberry	Tangerine	Taupe	Tourmaline
Tea Rose	Terra Cotta	Tawny	Willow
Tomato	Yam	Topaz	Wintergreen

Come Write with Me: POETRY Workbook & Journal (For Children) Vol. 1 | Brooke E. Wayne

BLUE   PURPLE   BROWN   OTHER

BLUE	PURPLE	BROWN	OTHER
Aqua	Amethyst	Beige	_____
Aquamarine	Blackberry	Cappuccino	_____
Azure	Concord	Caramel	_____
Baby Blue	Eggplant	Cedar	_____
Blueberry	Grape	Chestnut	_____
Cadet	Lavender	Chocolate	_____
Capri	Lilac	Coffee	_____
Caribbean	Mulberry	Fawn	_____
Cerulean	Orchid	Hazelnut	_____
Cobalt	Periwinkle	Hickory	_____
Cornflower	Plum	Leather	_____
Cyan	Violet	Mocha	_____
Denim		Nutmeg	_____
Indigo	**WHITE**	Sandalwood	_____
Iris		Sepia	_____
Larimar	Antique	Tan	_____
Midnight	Ash	Toffee	_____
Navy	Diamond	Walnut	_____
Ocean	Dove	Wheat	_____
Oxford	Eggshell		_____
Peacock	Frost	**BLACK**	_____
Persian	Ivory		_____
Powder	Marble	Charcoal	_____
Robin's Egg	Marshmallow	Granite	_____
Royal	Opal	Graphite	_____
Sapphire	Oyster	Gray	_____
Sea Foam	Pearl	Ink	_____
Sky	Platinum	Jet	_____
Teal	Porcelain	Onyx	_____
Tiffany	Silver	Pewter	_____
Topaz	Snow	Sable	_____
Turquoise	Sugar	Smoke	_____
Ultramarine	Vanilla	Steel	_____

PERSONALITY TRAITS & EMOTIONS

Adventurous	Fake	Knowledgeable	Popular	_____
Affectionate	Fancy	Kooky	Quaint	_____
Aggressive	Foolish	Laughable	Quick	_____
Altruistic	Forgetful	Lazy	Quiet	_____
Ambitious	Fortunate	Liberal	Quizzical	_____
Appropriate	Friendly	Logical	Radical	_____
Artistic	Funny	Lonely	Ravishing	_____
Blessed	Gallant	Loquacious	Realistic	_____
Boisterous	Gentle	Loud	Reclusive	_____
Boring	Giddy	Maddening	Reserved	_____
Brave	Gracious	Magical	Sad	_____
Brilliant	Guilty	Mature	Sappy	_____
Bubbly	Gullible	Merry	Sarcastic	_____
Caring	Happy	Mischievous	Serene	_____
Clever	Hasty	Mystical	Shy	_____
Comical	Hateful	Natural	Smart	_____
Courageous	Helpful	Naughty	Sophisticated	_____
Cowardly	Hesitant	Nefarious	Studious	_____
Crafty	Honest	Nervous	Subdued	_____
Creative	Humble	Nice	Talented	_____
Defensive	Hyperactive	Noble	Tenderhearted	_____
Depressed	Idealistic	Nonsensical	Thoughtful	_____
Discordant	Imaginative	Oblivious	Tormented	_____
Dreamy	Immature	Obnoxious	Tricky	_____
Dull	Innovative	Obsessive	Underrated	_____
Elated	Intelligent	Opinionated	Uppity	_____
Energetic	Introverted	Optimistic	Upset	_____
Ethical	Jealous	Outgoing	Visionary	_____
Excited	Jovial	Outlandish	Whimsical	_____
Expectant	Joyful	Outspoken	Wild	_____
Extravagant	Jubilant	Passive	Wise	_____
Extroverted	Keen	Pessimistic	Wistful	_____
Fabulous	Kind	Pleasing	Youthful	_____

COLOR ME

DIRECTIONS: On the following page, you will see the same poem as this one with all the fill-in-the-blank spaces awaiting your personal touch. Look through the Imagery, Color, and Personality Traits & Emotions Lists to find words that are meaningful to you. Then create your own Color Me poem. Once you complete the template, rewrite it again neatly on the journal page.

COLOR ME PURPLE

Color me purple
The color of royalty.
Don't shade me in a jealous, aggressive, dull green.
That's not who I am.
Color me lilac, lavender, orchid purple.
It's so much more my style.
I'm not a maddening, radical red,
Or a goofy, loud orange.
Just a quiet, friendly, sophisticated purple.
That's the color I'll be.
I'm the color of queen's cloaks
and starry skies,
The color of a juicy grape
bursting with sugary sunshine.
Color me caring,
Color me blessed.
I'm purple. That's what I am.
That's the color of me.

by
Brooke E. Wayne

COLOR ME _____
basic color

Color me _____
basic color

The color of _____.
abstract noun

Don't shade me in a _____, _____, _____ _____.
three unlike personality traits or emotions   unlike color

That's not who I am.

Color me _____, _____, _____ _____.
three different shades of the basic color   basic color

It's so much more my style.

I'm not a/an _____, _____, _____,
two unlike personality traits or emotions   unlike color

Or a/an _____, _____, _____.
two unlike personality traits or emotions   unlike color

Just a/an _____, _____, _____ _____.
three personality traits or emotions   basic color

That's the color I'll be.

I'm the color of _____
describe an object or a scene metaphorically

_____,

The color of a/an _____
describe an object or a scene metaphorically

_____.

Color me _____,
emotion

Color me _____.
emotion

I'm _____. That's what I am.
basic color

That's the color of me.

by

_____

_____

_____

_____

_____

_____

_____

_____

_____

_____

_____

_____

_____

_____

_____

_____

_____

_____

_____

_____

IMAGERY POETRY

Directions: This fill-in-the-blank poem uses several metaphors to create a poem about all your unique qualities and interests. See the example for ideas, as well as the Colors lists and Personality Traits & Emotions list on the previous pages, then add your own words to the lines. When you are done filling in all the blanks, rewrite your poem neatly on the blank page provided. Remember, you can always add or take away parts of the template to suit your personal style.

THEME: SEASON (Spring, Summer, Fall, Winter)

I chose Fall for my example on the next page.

RECAP ON POETIC DEVICES:

Imagery: sight, sound, smell, taste, touch (sensuous qualities)

Metaphor: a person, place, thing, or quality is compared directly to another person, place, thing, or quality

POEM STYLE: Free Verse (does not rhyme)

I am FALL through several lines of poetry that reflect my personality with objects related to that season.

I AM FALL

I shine brightly in
crimson, marigold, and hickory.
Look around, and you'll see
falling leaves, mud puddles, and cloudy skies.
Listen closely, and you'll hear
the howling wind.
Now, take a breath, and you will smell
fresh rain and cinnamon.
If you poured me into a cup and drank from it,
you would taste hot apple cider,
or reached out your hand,
you would touch a brittle leaf.
I am
cozy campfires and toasted marshmallows.
I am Fall.

by

Brooke E. Wayne

I AM _____
season

I shine brightly in
_____, _____, and _____.

list three colors you would see in your season

Look around, and you'll see
_____.

describe things that belong in your season

Listen closely, and you'll hear
_____.

describe things you would hear in your season

Now, take a breath, and you will smell
_____.

describe things you would smell in your season

If you poured me into a cup and drank from it, you would taste _____,

describe a popular drink in your season

or reached out your hand, you would touch _____.

describe things you would touch in your season

I am
_____.

describe things that belong in your season

I am _____.
season

by

_____

your name

Write

_____

_____

_____

_____

_____

_____

_____

_____

_____

_____

_____

_____

_____

_____

_____

_____

_____

_____

_____

BORING TO BRILLIANT

DIRECTIONS: You will turn a boring starter prompt into a brilliant poem.

Do you notice how the boring poem starter below has five syllables per line and reads with a monotonous cadence?
(Syllables = word parts, Monotonous = repetitive, Cadence = rhythmic sound)
You will write poetry based on a few prompts, turning the boring starters into works of literary art that have varying sentence structures and lengths. By doing this, it creates a musical effect when a poem is being read.

I created a Brilliant Revamp of the first Boring Starter Prompt for you on the next page for you to study. Compare the two writings, and see if you can identify all the poetic devices and words from the lists that I used to write the new and improved poem. Then begin your own Brilliant Poetry using the other prompt starters.

Be sure to include as many details from the Imagery, Colors, and Personality Traits & Emotions lists as you can into your poetry.

BORING STARTER PROMPT:

The playground was large.

It had water spouts.

The weather was hot.

I played for hours.

BORING TO BRILLIANT

The Playground

The playground was a jungle
of canary, lime, and plum
painted metal bars.

Waterspouts even erupted from the ground
like broken fire hydrants.

The scorching sun
poured molten lava rays
down on all of us playing.

For hours, we laughed and screamed,
having fun on the structures
between soaking ourselves to keep cool!

by

Brooke E. Wayne

BORING TO BRILLIANT

Boring Starter Prompt

**I went to the amusement park.
It had all kinds of rides.
I screamed on the rollercoaster.
It was really fun.**

_____

_____

_____

_____

_____

_____

_____

_____

_____

_____

by

_____

Boring Starter Prompt

I went to the carnival.
I ate all kinds of foods.
The clowns were scary.
There were lots of games and rides.

_____

_____

_____

_____

_____

_____

_____

_____

_____

_____

by

_____

BORING TO BRILLIANT

Boring Starter Prompt

I took a rocket to the planet.
There were creatures living there.
I learned about their lives.
Everything looked different there.

_____

_____

_____

_____

_____

_____

_____

_____

_____

by

_____

BORING TO BRILLIANT

Boring Starter Prompt

I got a new pet.
My pet likes to do crazy things.
I am teaching my pet tricks.
I love my new pet.

_____

_____

_____

_____

_____

_____

_____

_____

_____

by

_____

BORING TO BRILLIANT

Boring Starter Prompt

The sun came up over the ocean.
It was bright.
I saw dolphins in the waves.
The sky was pretty.

_____

_____

_____

_____

_____

_____

_____

_____

by

_____

Structured Poetry

Hey? Psst! Throughout the years,
many writers have created poems
that have specific structures to follow.
Whether the poem
has a special rhyme scheme
(see Literary Terms
at the beginning of the workbook
for a definition of rhyme scheme),
or the poem has a strict format
that includes certain words,
these types of poems are exciting to write!
Sometimes, the easiest way
to begin writing poetry
is to start with one that comes with rules.
Some of these structured poems
have been created by poets
who lived hundreds of years ago.
Some of these poetry types
have been around so long
no one knows who invented them.
Others are playful poems I added
to help you think creatively
with as little stress as possible.
No matter what,
I want you to do your personal best,
and add some poetic devices,
stretching your imagination
as you explore structured poetry.

STRUCTURED POETRY

ABC

ACROSTIC

SHAPE

CLASSIC CINQUAIN

MODERN CINQUAIN

HAIKU

TANKA

DIAMANTE

BLACKOUT

ABC POEM

Directions: An ABC Poem is a poem that starts each line out with the letters of the alphabet. You can see by the partial example below that you are allowed to break a line in two and use the next letter to finish the thought. Good luck with X! Maybe try breaking up a word like eXtra, if xylophone or x-ray doesn't fit into your poem's theme!

holidays
games
super heroes
birthday party
school
friends
outerspace
music
summer
technology
movies
wild animals
vacation
history
earth
people
feelings
fast food
sports
favorite
foods
pets
books
amusement parks
TV
family

EXAMPLE: FRUIT

Apples are a delicious fruit, but

Bananas are way better!

Creamy, sweet smoothies start with bananas and end with yum!

Did you know olives are considered a fruit, too?

Everything about pineapples, mangoes, and limes makes me think of ⋯

ABC POEM

A _____

B _____

C _____

D _____

E _____

F _____

G _____

H _____

I _____

J _____

K _____

L _____

M _____

N _____

O _____

P _____

Q _____

R _____

S _____

T _____

U _____

V _____

W _____

X _____

Y _____

Z _____

ACROSTIC POEM

Directions: In an Acrostic Poem, much like an ABC Poem, you write lines of poetry with the first word of each line starting with a specific letter. For this particular poem, the letters form a word, like your name or a specific theme. Of course, the whole poem is about that theme. For the example, I use my name and write about myself. If you choose to do your name, too, be sure to use some words to describe yourself from the Personality Traits & Emotions lists like I did.

B ubbly personality, always wearing a smile

R eads books and writes them, too

O ptimistic about life and is rarely

O utlandish, but more of a quiet person

K eeping calm and spreading hope to

E veryone, including students and friends

ACROSTIC POEM

_____

_____

_____

_____

_____

_____

_____

_____

_____

_____

_____

_____

_____

_____

_____

_____

_____

_____

SHAPE POEM

Directions: A Shape Poem is usually written in free-verse, which means it cannot rhyme. The poem's unique quality is that the words you write to compose your poem are arranged into a shape that represents the theme or an element of the poem itself.

Here is a simple example of a line in a Shape Poem.

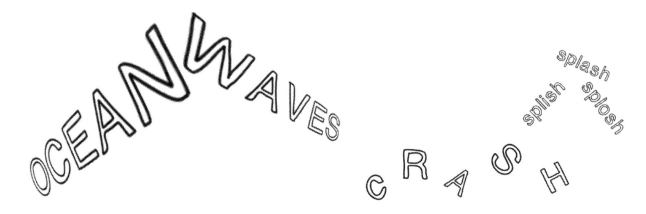

Add several possible themes and shapes to the brainstorming bubble for you to use in your own free-verse Shape Poem.

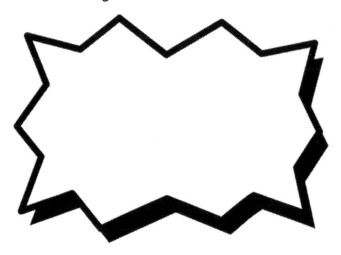

SHAPE POEM

CLASSIC CINQUAIN POEM

Directions: Adelaide Crapsey, who lived between 1878-1914, created the classic Cinquain Poem. It is a five-line stanza, which has set rules. The rules are each line must have a certain amount of syllables.

Syllables are word parts that make up a whole word. For example, beautiful is broken up into syllables like this: beau-ti-ful. Beautiful is a three syllable word.

It doesn't matter how many words make up a single line, as long as the total syllables in each line are in the amount required.

Classic Cinquain poetry follows this format:

Line 1: two syllables

Line 2: four syllables

Line 3: six syllables

Line 4: eight syllables

Line 5: two syllables

(Syllabic Pattern: 2-4-6-8-2)

CLASSIC CINQUAIN POEM

November Night

Listen ...

With faint dry sound

Like steps or passing ghosts,

The leaves, frost-crisp'd, break from the trees

And fall.

by
Adelaide Crapsey

Adelaide Crapsey's Cinquain poem, "November Night", follows the five-line format with specific syllabic counts per line. She adds lots of sensuous imagery, such as the phrase **faint dry sound**, which taps into touch and sound imagery, as well as the falling **leaves** giving the reader sight imagery. She even slips in a simile with the sound of the falling **leaves** being like the steps of **passing ghosts**.

CLASSIC CINQUAIN POEM

_____

_____

_____

_____

_____

_____

_____

_____

_____

_____

_____

_____

_____

_____

_____

_____

_____

_____

_____

MODERN CINQUAIN POEM

Directions: The modern Cinquain poem has five lines and follows a specific format, but, unlike the classic Cinquain, syllables do not play a part in this adaptation. The modern Cinquain focuses on specific types of words, as well as specific numbers of those words for each line. See the format below.

Line 1: one word
(theme)
*Capitalize this word

Line 2: two adjectives
(describing the theme)

Line 3: three verbs
("ing" action words about the theme)

Line 4: four words as a phrase
(expressing your feelings about the theme)

Line 5: one word synonym
(another word for the theme)
*Capitalize this word

MODERN CINQUAIN POEM

Example of a modern Cinquain poem:

Books

digital   **paperback**

reading   **discovering**   **imagining**

lose   **myself**   **to**   **adventure**

Novels

MODERN CINQUAIN POEM

_____

_____ _____

_____ _____ _____

_____ _____ _____

_____

HAIKU POEM

Directions: A Haiku Poem is a Japanese poem that celebrates nature. It is composed of three lines. Each line has a specifc amount of syllables. The first line has five syllables, the second line has seven syllables, and the third line has five syllables. For a modern twist, you can write about any theme you want to, but it must follow the 5-7-5 rule about syllables.

Here are some 5 syllable lines and 7 syllable lines for you to use to create some practice poems with on the next page.

5 Syllable Lines:

spring begins to bloom
sharp glowing embers
glittery starlight
sunshine warms the cove

7 Syllable Lines:

stirring my soul to be free
captures my heart with its song
catching my eye from afar
from a distance calls to me

5 Syllable Lines:

shattered by the sun
with a cool whisper
on this new journey
like a gentle breeze

HAIKU POEM

Directions: I created an example out of the lines on the previous page. Now it's your turn. Create a few nature-themed Haiku Poems using the lines I've provided for you, or come up with your own words that follow the syllabic rules. You can alter any of the words if you need to, just make sure the syllables stay the same. On the following page, write several Haiku Poems about nature or any theme you want to.

Glittery starlight
Catching my eye from afar
With a cool whisper

They are so fluffy,
~~They are~~

They are so gentle and cute,

They are the best cats!

My pappa is great,

He is the best one of all!

Pappa ~~kow~~ knows whats best!

HAIKU POEM

The brush weed is swift,

It swayes with the blowing wind...

but what is the oac?

TANKA POEM

Directions: Much like a Haiku Poem, a Tanka Poem has a set number of lines with specific amounts of syllables assigned to each line. The format is five lines of poetry with a syllabic count of 5-7-5-7-7. Unlike a Haiku Poem, though, a Tanka Poem focuses on emotional experiences and themes that do not revolve around nature. You will see some practice lines below with five and seven syllables each for you to use and/or tweak as needed.

5 Syllable Lines

I care about you
Cherishing our time
Loving is easy
Walks with my mother
Hope is an anchor
Quiet moments shared
Once in a blue moon
Soft words are spoken

7 Syllable Lines

The world seems so far away
Truth comes to light in your heart
Some friendships last forever
We always have each other
Memories are being made
We laugh and share our secrets
What a sight for us to see
Everything fills me with joy

TANKA POEM

Directions: Below, you can see an example of a Tanka Poem using some of the premade lines from the previous page. Create a practice Tanka Poem, too. If you alter any of the premade lines to suit your style, be sure to maintain the 5-7-5-7-7 syllabic count pattern.

**Cherishing our time
the world seems so far away
quiet moments shared
we laugh and spill our secrets
some friendships last forever**

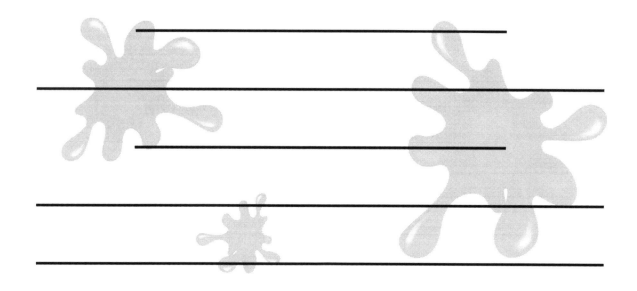

TANKA POEM

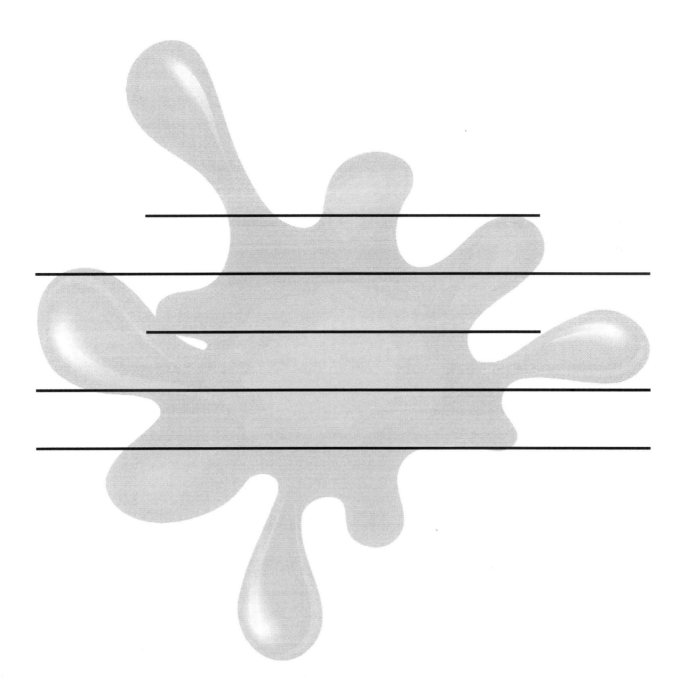

DIAMANTE POEM

Directions: A Diamante Poem creates the shape of a baseball diamond. In general, poems that look like a specific image are also called Shape Poems. Each line of a Diamante Poem has specific rules that must be followed. Below, you will see the rules. On the following pages, you will also see a fill-in-the-blank to create your own Diamante Poem.

TIP: When writing a Diamante Poem, do Line 1 and Line 7 first!

Line 1: One noun--theme

Line 2: Two adjectives describing the Line 1 theme

Line 3: Three "ing" action words related to Line 1 theme

Line 4: Two synonyms (similar words) to the Line 1 theme and two synonyms (similar words) to the Line 7 theme

Line 5: Three "ing action words related to Line 7 theme

Line 6: Two adjectives describing the Line 7 theme

Line 7: One antonym (opposite) of the Line 1 theme

DIAMANTE POEM

This poem is an example of a Diamonte Poem.
The theme I chose is SUNRISE.
Notice how the poem is split in the middle in line 4
after the word 'morning',
and everything after that word is all about
the opposite word SUNSET.

Sunrise
shiny, colorful
rising, welcoming, warming
daybreak, morning, evening, nightfall
setting, slumbering, cooling
vibrant, beautiful
Sunset

DIAMANTE POEM

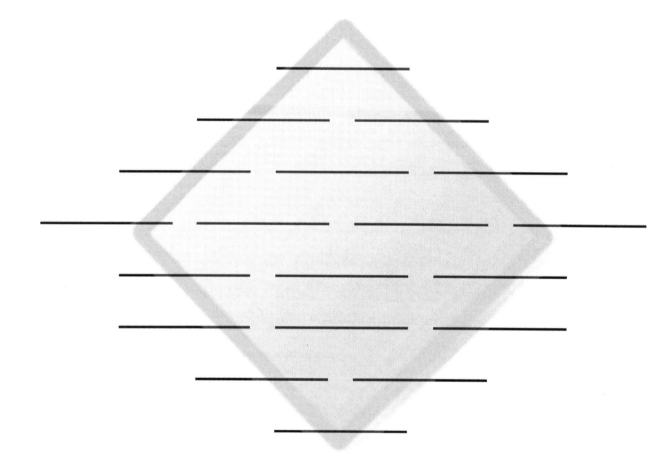

BLACKOUT POEM

Directions: Create a poem by picking out words and phrases you like on the book page. Black out all the other words on the page you don't want in your poem, showing only the unique poem you created with those chosen words. You can also create shapes or an artistic picture to cover up the extra words, instead of just scribbling over them like the example.

For several months, Belle lived a life of luxury at the Beast's palace, having every whim catered to by servants, with no end of riches to amuse her and an endless supply of exquisite finery to wear. Eventually she became homesick and begged the Beast to allow her to go to see her family. He allowed it on the condition that she would return exactly a week later. Belle agreed to this and set off for home with an enchanted mirror and ring. The mirror allowed her to see what was going on back at the Beast's castle, and the ring allowed her to return to the castle in an instant when turned three times around her finger. Her older sisters were surprised to find her well fed and dressed in finery. They were envious when they heard of her happy life at the castle, and, hearing that she must return to the Beast on a certain day, begged her to stay another day, even putting onion in their eyes to make it appear as though they were weeping. They hoped that the Beast would be angry with Belle for breaking her promise and would eat her alive. Belle's heart was moved by her sisters' false show of love, and she agreed to stay.

Belle began to feel guilty about breaking her promise to the Beast and used the mirror to see

Beauty and the Beast excerpt, courtesy of public domain children's books.

THE VELVETEEN RABBIT

"Real isn't how you are made," said the Skin Horse.

"It's a thing that happens to you.

When a child loves you

for a long, long time,

not just to play with,

but REALLY loves you,

then you become Real."

"Does it happen all at once,

like being wound up," the Rabbit asked,

"or bit by bit?"

"It doesn't happen all at once," said the Skin Horse.

"You become.

It takes a long time.

Generally, by the time you are Real,

most of your hair has been loved off,

and your eyes drop out

and you get loose in the joints and very shabby.

But these things don't matter at all,

because once you are Real you can't be ugly,

except to people who don't understand."

Excerpt from *The Velveteen Rabbit*
by Margery Williams

ALICE'S ADVENTURES IN WONDERLAND

"It was much pleasanter at home," thought poor Alice, "when one wasn't always growing larger and smaller, and being ordered about by mice and rabbits. I almost wish I hadn't gone down that rabbit-hole—and yet—and yet—it's rather curious, you know, this sort of life! I do wonder what *can* have happened to me! When I used to read fairy-tales, I fancied that kind of thing never happened, and now here I am in the middle of one! There ought to be a book written about me, that there ought! And when I grow up, I'll write one—but I'm grown up now," she added in a sorrowful tone, "at least there's no room to grow up any more *here*."

"But then," thought Alice, "shall I never get any older than I am now? That'll be a comfort, one way—never to be an old woman—but then—always to have lessons to learn! Oh, I shouldn't like *that*!"

"Oh, you foolish Alice!" she answered herself. "How can you learn lessons in here? Why, there's hardly room for you, and no room at all for any lesson-books!"

And so she went on, taking first one side and then the other, and making quite a conversation of it altogether, but after a few minutes she heard a voice outside, and stopped to listen.

Excerpt from *Alice's Adventures in Wonderland*
By Lewis Carroll

"A library is a good place

To go when you feel unhappy,

For there, in a book,

You may find encouragement and comfort.

A library is a good place to go

When you feel bewildered or undecided,

For there, in a book,

You may have your question answered.

Books are good company,

In sad times and happy times,

For books are people—

People who have managed to stay alive

By hiding between the covers

Of a book."

E. B. White
Author of Charlotte's Web

THE WIND IN THE WILLOWS

"There you are!" cried the Toad, straddling and expanding himself. "There's real life for you, embodied in that little cart. The open road, the dusty highway, the heath, the common, the hedgerows, the rolling downs! Camps, villages, towns, cities! Here today, up and off to somewhere else to-morrow! Travel, change, interest, excitement! The whole world before you, and a horizon that's always changing! And mind! This is the very first cart of its sort that was ever built, without any exception. Come inside and look at the arrangements. Planned 'em all myself, I did!"

The Mole was tremendously interested and excited, and followed him eagerly up the steps and into the interior of the caravan. The Rat only snorted and thrust his hands deep into his pockets, remaining where he was.

It was indeed very compact and comfortable. Little sleeping bunks—a little table that folded up against the wall—a cooking-stove, lockers, bookshelves, a birdcage with a bird in it; and pots, pan, jugs, and kettles of every size and variety.

"All complete!" said the Toad triumphantly, pulling open a locker. "You see biscuits, potted lobster, sardines—everything you can possibly want. Soda-water here—baccy there—a letter-paper, bacon, jam, cards and dominoes—you'll find," he continued, as they descended the steps again. "You'll find that nothing whatever has been forgotten, when we make our start this afternoon."

"I beg your pardon," said the Rat slowly, as he chewed a straw, "but did I overhear you say something about "we," and "start," and "this afternoon?"

"Now, you dear good old Ratty," said Toad, imploringly, "don't begin talking in that stiff and sniffy sort of way, because you know you've got to come. I can't possibly manage without you, so please consider it settled, and don't argue—it's the one thing I can't stand. You surely don't mean to stick to your dull fusty old river all your life, and just live in a hole in a bank, and boat? I want to show you the World! I'm going to make an animal of you, my boy!"

"I don't care," said the Rat, doggedly. "I'm not coming, and that's flat. And I am going to stick to my old river, and live in a hole, and boat, as I've always done. And what's more, Mole's going to stick to me and do as I do, aren't you, Mole?"

Excerpt from *The Wind in the Willows*
By Kenneth Grahame

Blackout Poem

Directions: Find a newspaper, magazine, or old book, then tear out a section and glue it here. Then create your own Blackout Poem on it.

Prompts

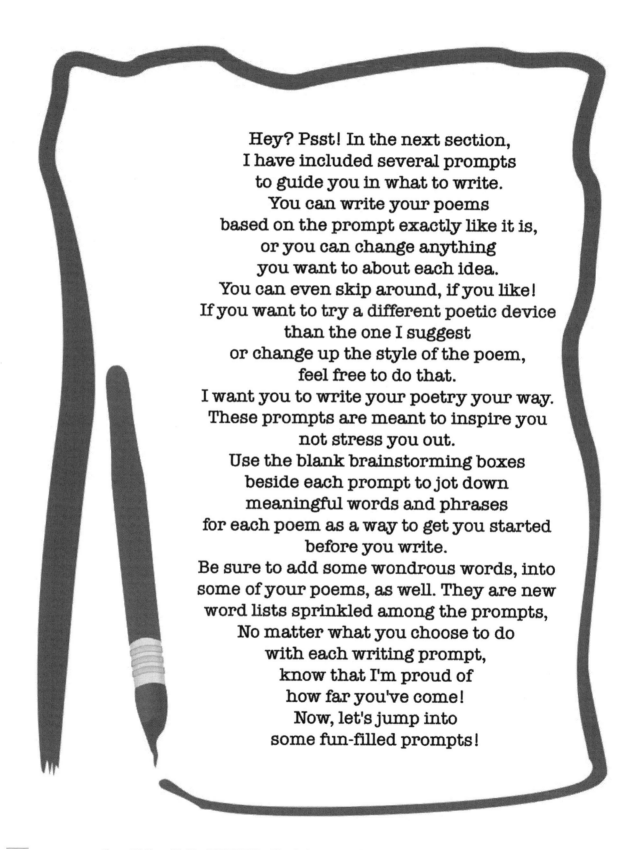

Hey? Psst! In the next section,
I have included several prompts
to guide you in what to write.
You can write your poems
based on the prompt exactly like it is,
or you can change anything
you want to about each idea.
You can even skip around, if you like!
If you want to try a different poetic device
than the one I suggest
or change up the style of the poem,
feel free to do that.
I want you to write your poetry your way.
These prompts are meant to inspire you
not stress you out.
Use the blank brainstorming boxes
beside each prompt to jot down
meaningful words and phrases
for each poem as a way to get you started
before you write.
Be sure to add some wondrous words, into
some of your poems, as well. They are new
word lists sprinkled among the prompts,
No matter what you choose to do
with each writing prompt,
know that I'm proud of
how far you've come!
Now, let's jump into
some fun-filled prompts!

Brainstorming Box:
Fill this space with your pre-writing words, phrases,
and lines for the next section.

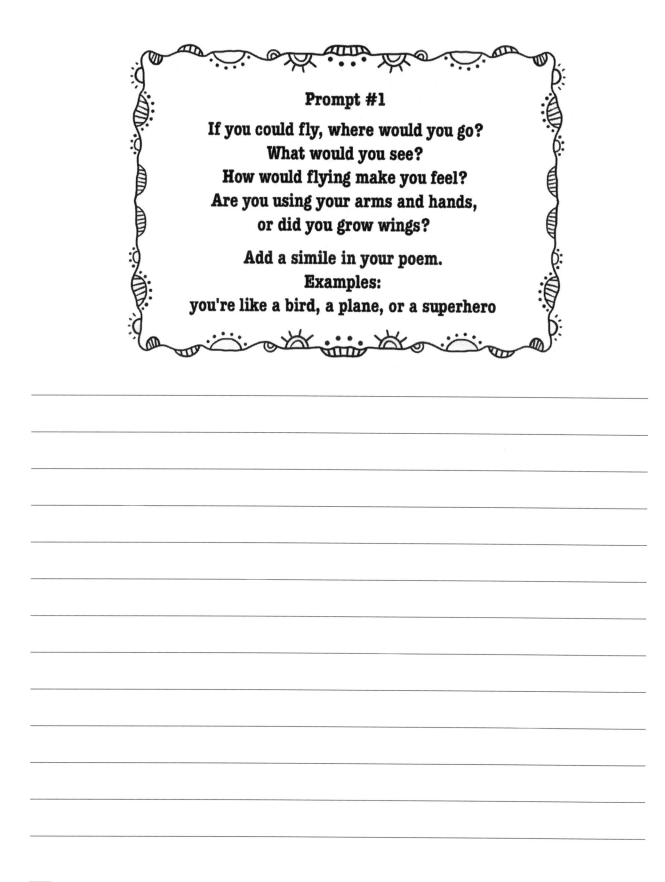

Prompt #1

If you could fly, where would you go?
What would you see?
How would flying make you feel?
Are you using your arms and hands,
or did you grow wings?

Add a simile in your poem.
Examples:
you're like a bird, a plane, or a superhero

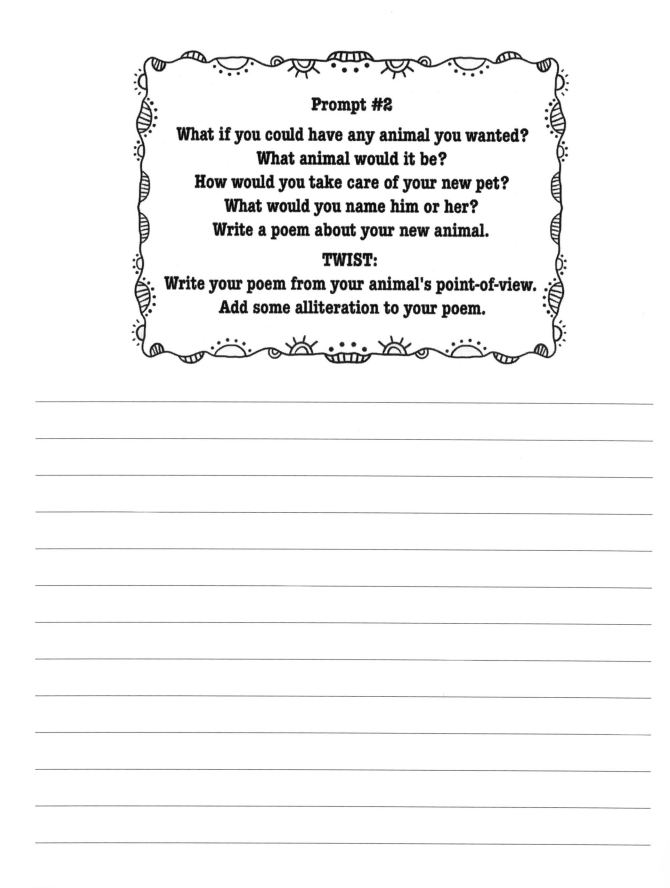

Prompt #2

What if you could have any animal you wanted?
What animal would it be?
How would you take care of your new pet?
What would you name him or her?
Write a poem about your new animal.

TWIST:

Write your poem from your animal's point-of-view.
Add some alliteration to your poem.

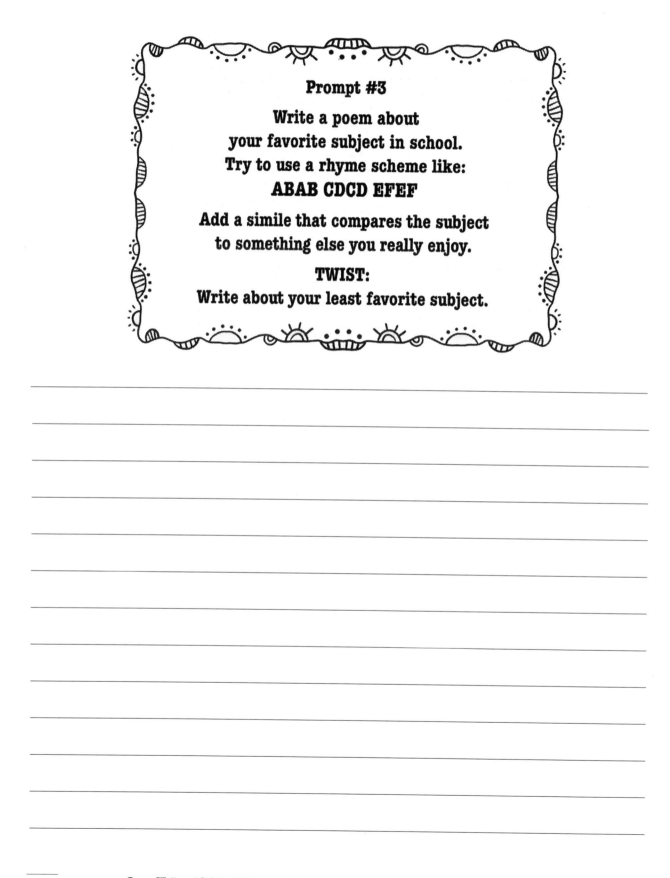

Prompt #3

Write a poem about
your favorite subject in school.
Try to use a rhyme scheme like:

ABAB CDCD EFEF

Add a simile that compares the subject
to something else you really enjoy.

TWIST:

Write about your least favorite subject.

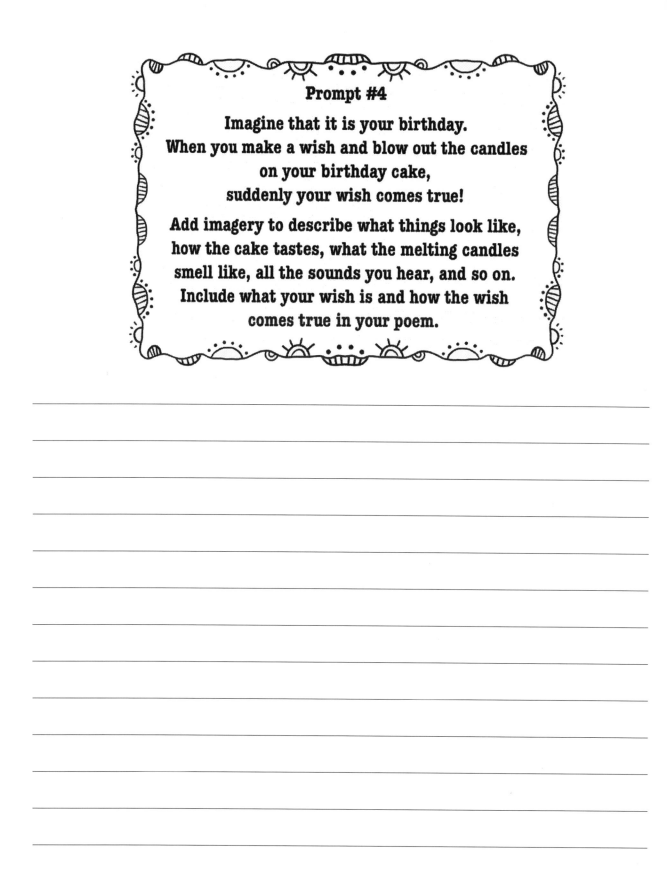

Prompt #4

Imagine that it is your birthday.
When you make a wish and blow out the candles
on your birthday cake,
suddenly your wish comes true!

Add imagery to describe what things look like,
how the cake tastes, what the melting candles
smell like, all the sounds you hear, and so on.
Include what your wish is and how the wish
comes true in your poem.

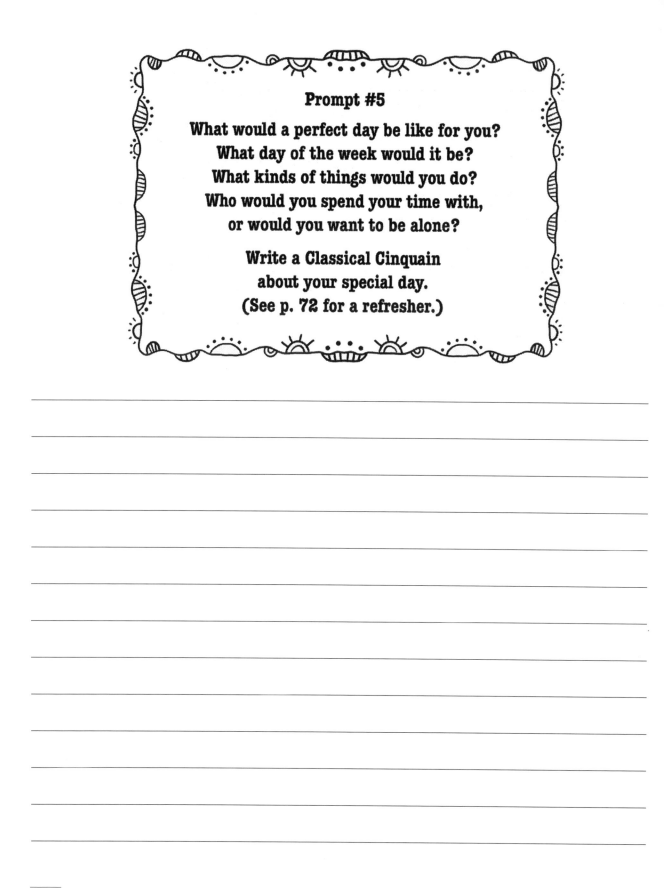

Prompt #5

What would a perfect day be like for you?
What day of the week would it be?
What kinds of things would you do?
Who would you spend your time with,
or would you want to be alone?

Write a Classical Cinquain
about your special day.
(See p. 72 for a refresher.)

Wondrous Words

SMARTER SYNONYMS FOR SIMPLE WORDS

COLD:
Chilly, Frigid, Freezing

DARK:
Gloomy, Shadowy, Dismal

HOT:
Smoldering, Scorching, Fiery

LOOK:
Gaze, Glance, Glare

MAKE:
Invent, Create, Manifest

PEACE:
Tranquility, Repose, Serene

SMALL:
Minuscule, Petite, Slight

SPEAK:
Shout, Whisper, Utter

TAKE:
Clutch, Possess, Capture

WALK:
Jaunt, Stroll, Saunter

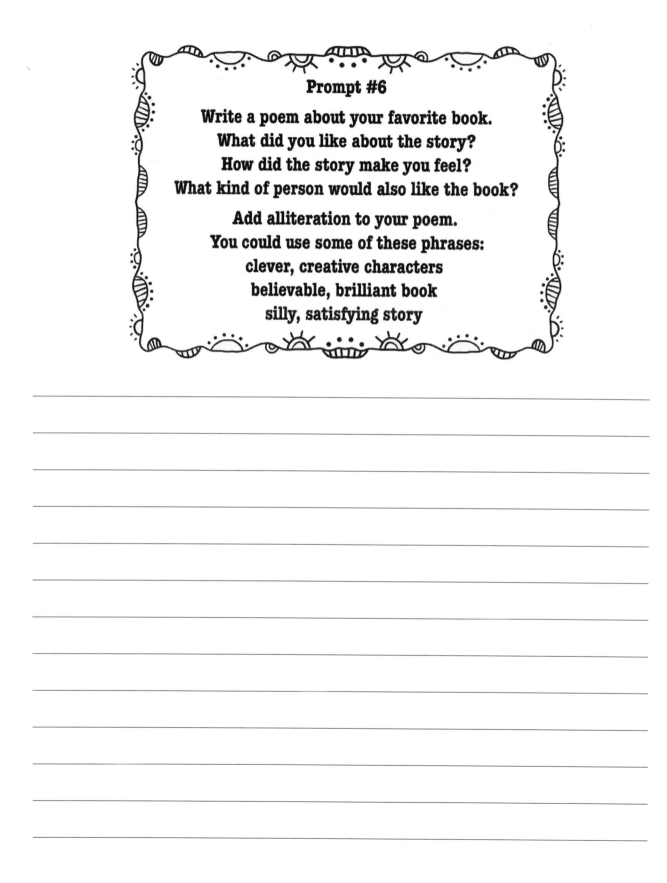

Prompt #6

Write a poem about your favorite book.
What did you like about the story?
How did the story make you feel?
What kind of person would also like the book?

Add alliteration to your poem.
You could use some of these phrases:
clever, creative characters
believable, brilliant book
silly, satisfying story

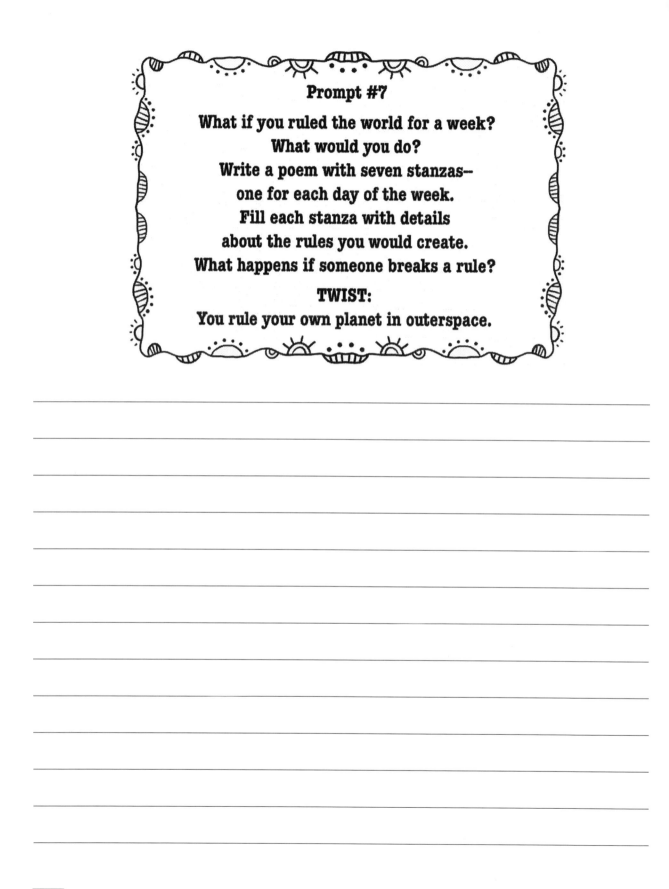

Prompt #7

What if you ruled the world for a week?
What would you do?
Write a poem with seven stanzas--
one for each day of the week.
Fill each stanza with details
about the rules you would create.
What happens if someone breaks a rule?

TWIST:
You rule your own planet in outerspace.

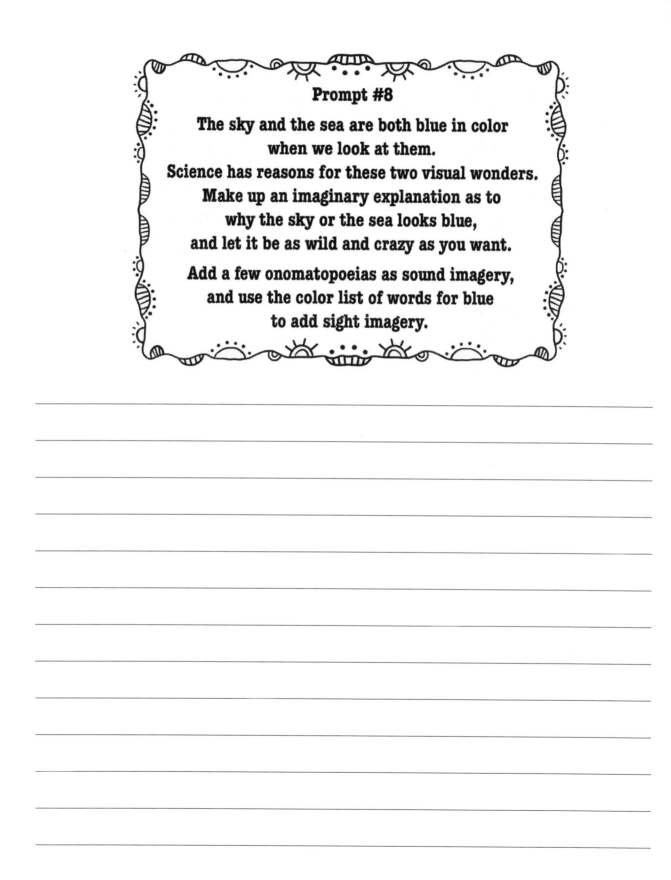

Prompt #8

The sky and the sea are both blue in color
when we look at them.
Science has reasons for these two visual wonders.
Make up an imaginary explanation as to
why the sky or the sea looks blue,
and let it be as wild and crazy as you want.

Add a few onomatopoeias as sound imagery,
and use the color list of words for blue
to add sight imagery.

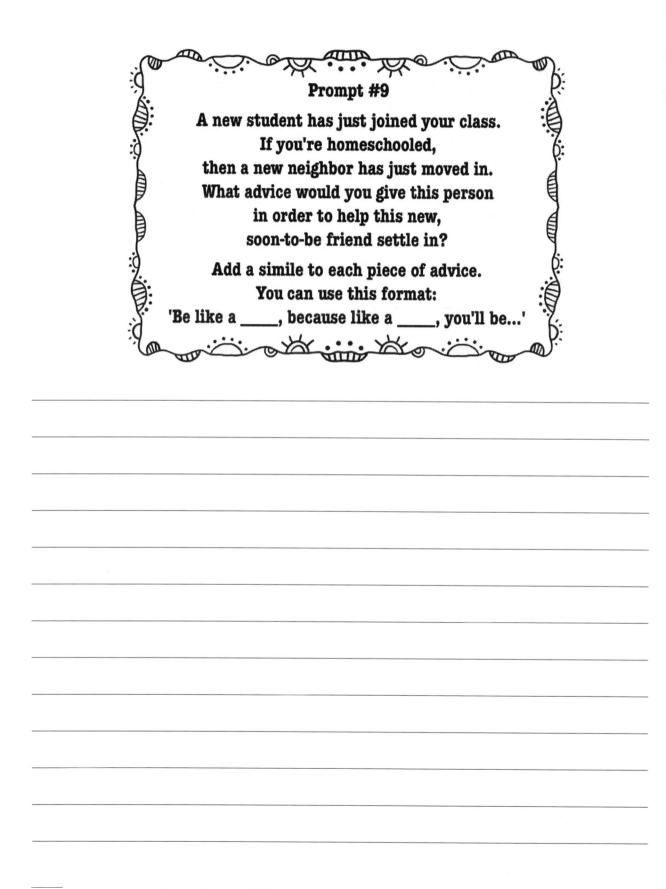

Prompt #9

A new student has just joined your class.
If you're homeschooled,
then a new neighbor has just moved in.
What advice would you give this person
in order to help this new,
soon-to-be friend settle in?

Add a simile to each piece of advice.
You can use this format:
'Be like a _____, because like a _____, you'll be...'

Wondrous Words

THE FOUR ELEMENTS

EARTH:

Trees
(Willow, Oak, Cherry, Fig, etc.)
Flowers
(Rose, Carnation, Daisy, Milk Thistle, etc.)
Vegetation
(Dandelion, Tumbleweed, Grass, Cactus, etc.)
Crops
(Wheat, Alfalfa, Grape Vines, Artichokes, Peanuts, Potatoes, etc.)

FIRE:

Campfire, Bonfire, Candle Flame, Torch
Ash, Charcoal, Soot, Gas Stove, Log Stove
Volcanic Lava, Magma, Inferno, Blaze, Ember, Cinder

WATER:

Lake, Pond, Marsh
Ocean, Sea, Tide, Wave
Lagoon, Bay, Bayou, Gulf
Mist, Vapor, Cloud, Rain
Puddle, Raindrop, Quagmire
Steam, Fog, Dew, Drizzle, Gloom
Hurricane, Typhoon, Rain Storm, Squall

AIR:

Breeze, Jet, Current
Zephyr, Cyclone, Gale
Tornado, Thunder Storm
Draft, Whirlwind, Flurry, Waft, Gust

Brainstorming Box:
Fill this space with your pre-writing words, phrases,
and lines for the next section.

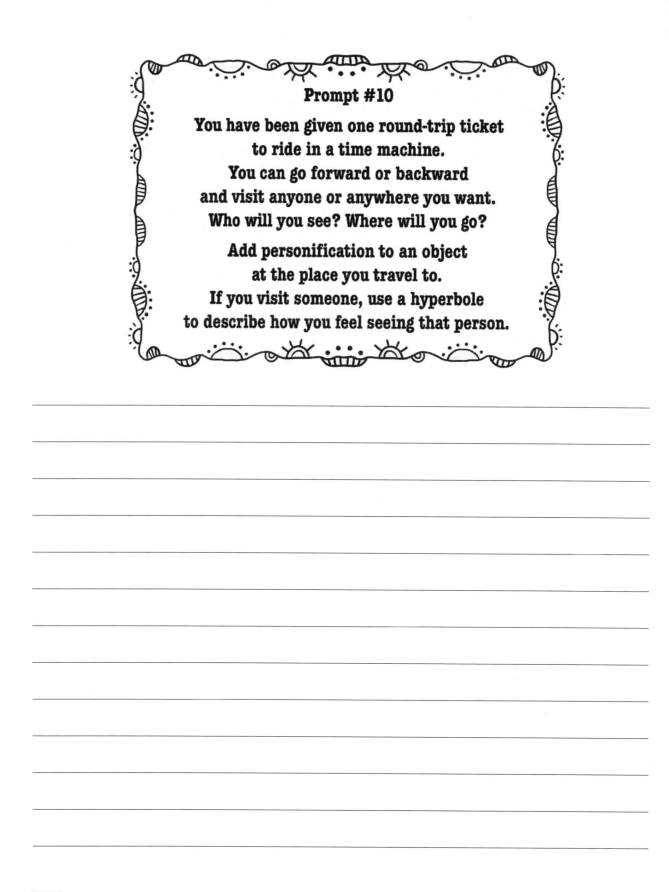

Prompt #10

You have been given one round-trip ticket
to ride in a time machine.
You can go forward or backward
and visit anyone or anywhere you want.
Who will you see? Where will you go?

Add personification to an object
at the place you travel to.
If you visit someone, use a hyperbole
to describe how you feel seeing that person.

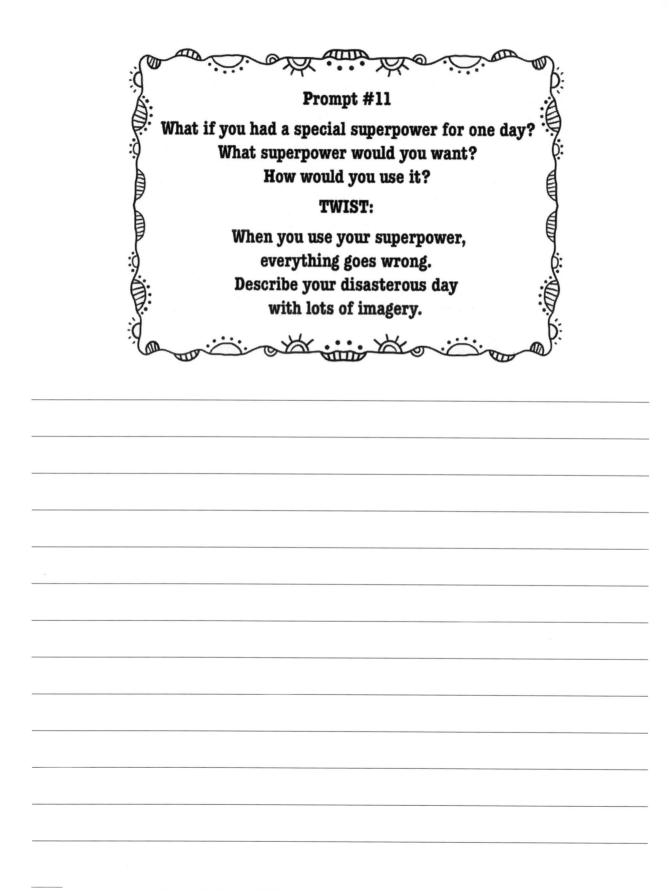

Prompt #11

What if you had a special superpower for one day?
What superpower would you want?
How would you use it?

TWIST:

When you use your superpower,
everything goes wrong.
Describe your disasterous day
with lots of imagery.

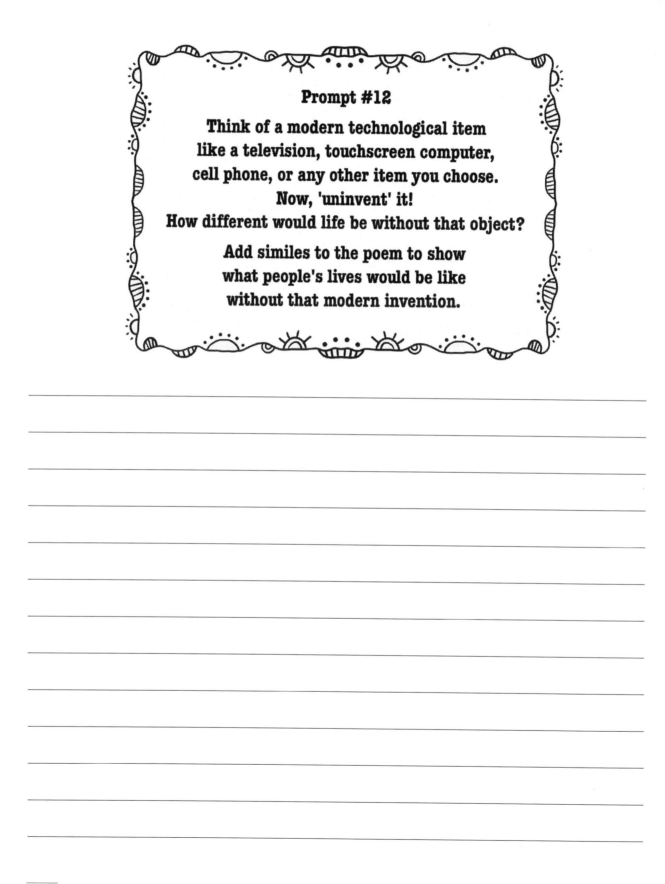

Prompt #12

Think of a modern technological item
like a television, touchscreen computer,
cell phone, or any other item you choose.
Now, 'uninvent' it!
How different would life be without that object?

Add similes to the poem to show
what people's lives would be like
without that modern invention.

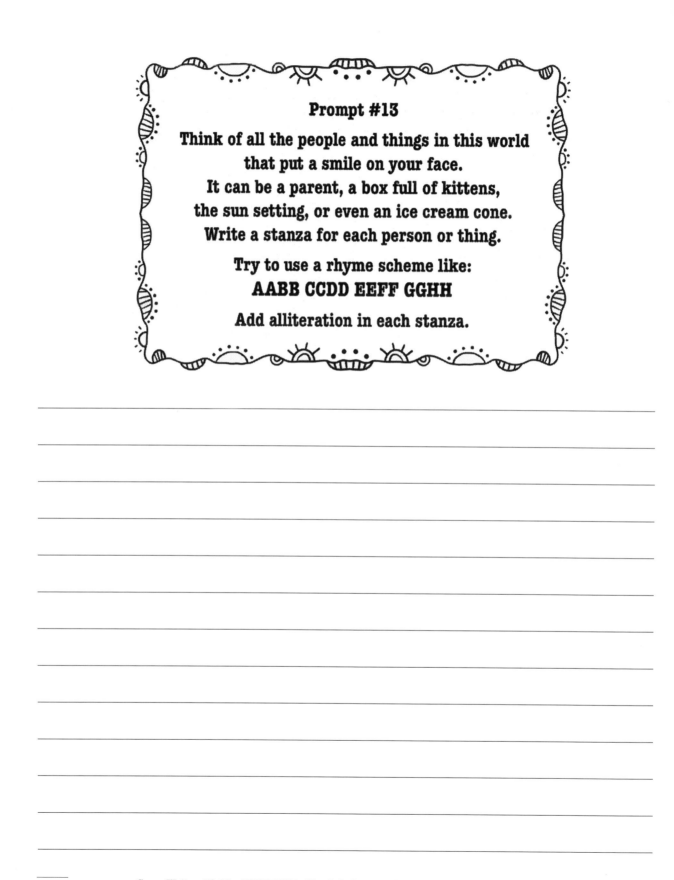

Prompt #13

Think of all the people and things in this world
that put a smile on your face.
It can be a parent, a box full of kittens,
the sun setting, or even an ice cream cone.
Write a stanza for each person or thing.

Try to use a rhyme scheme like:
AABB CCDD EEFF GGHH

Add alliteration in each stanza.

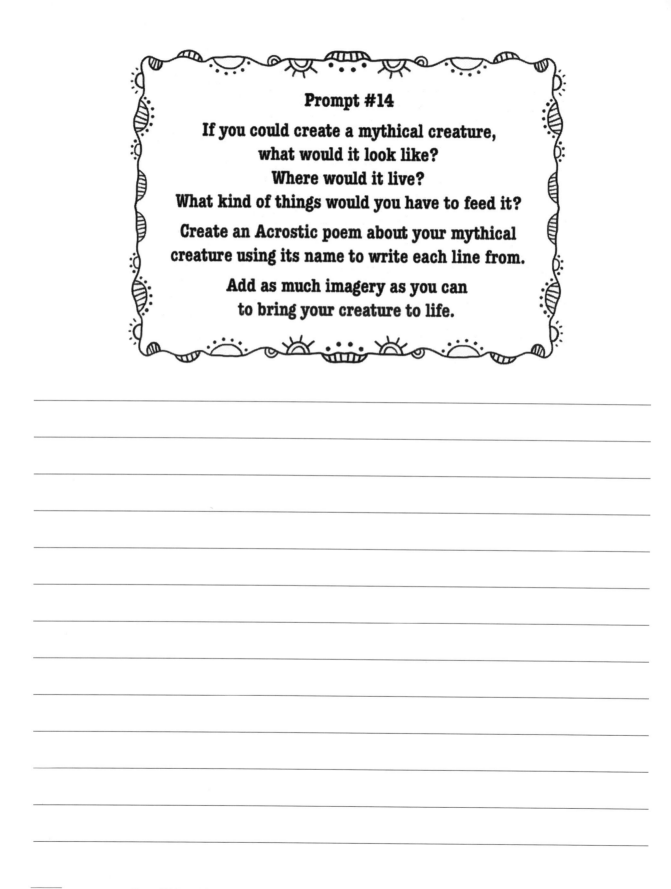

Prompt #14

If you could create a mythical creature,
what would it look like?

Where would it live?

What kind of things would you have to feed it?

Create an Acrostic poem about your mythical
creature using its name to write each line from.

Add as much imagery as you can
to bring your creature to life.

Wondrous Words

RHYMING WORDS

Short 'an' Rhymes:
Can, Ran, Man, Plan, Van, Fan

Short 'e' Rhymes:
Bed, Led, Red, Shed, Ahead

Short 'i' Rhymes:
Sit, Lit, Bit, Hit, Mitt, Pit, Wit

Short 'o' Rhymes:
Rot, Pot, Not, Hot, Dot, Cot

Short 'u' Rhymes:
Hug, Pug, Rug, Lug, Dug, Bug, Mug

Rhyming Sets:

Splinter, Winter
Space, Place, Race
Small, Tall, All, Call
Crazy, Lazy, Daisy, Hazy
Show, Grow, Know, Glow, Go
Here, Hear, Near, Dear, Shear, Clear
Light, Night, Bright, Height, Fight, Right

RHYMING RESOURCES:

www.rhymedb.com
www.rhymezone.com
www.rhymes.net
www.wikirhymer.com

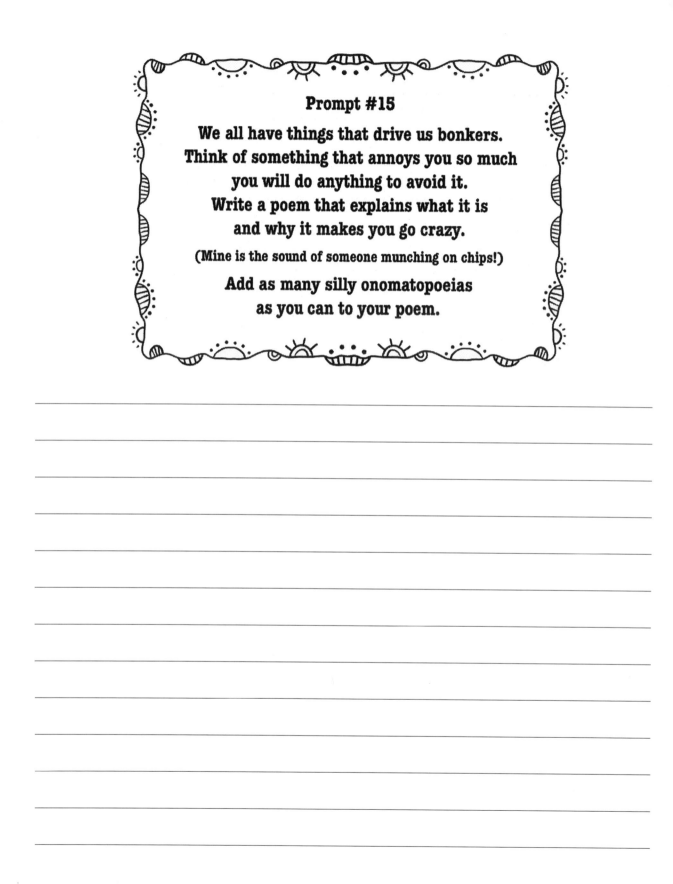

Prompt #15

We all have things that drive us bonkers.
Think of something that annoys you so much
you will do anything to avoid it.
Write a poem that explains what it is
and why it makes you go crazy.

(Mine is the sound of someone munching on chips!)

Add as many silly onomatopoeias
as you can to your poem.

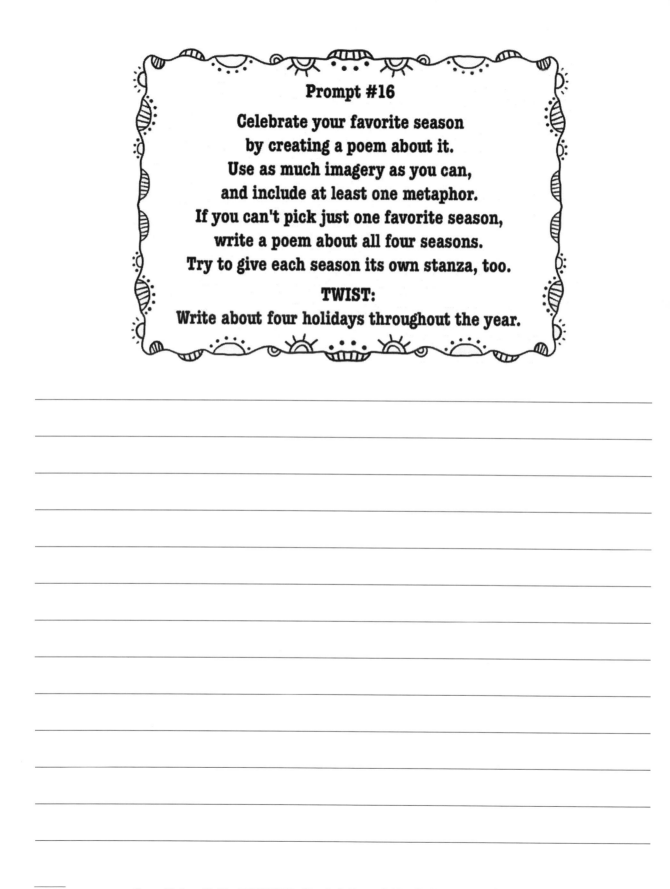

Prompt #16

Celebrate your favorite season
by creating a poem about it.
Use as much imagery as you can,
and include at least one metaphor.
If you can't pick just one favorite season,
write a poem about all four seasons.
Try to give each season its own stanza, too.

TWIST:

Write about four holidays throughout the year.

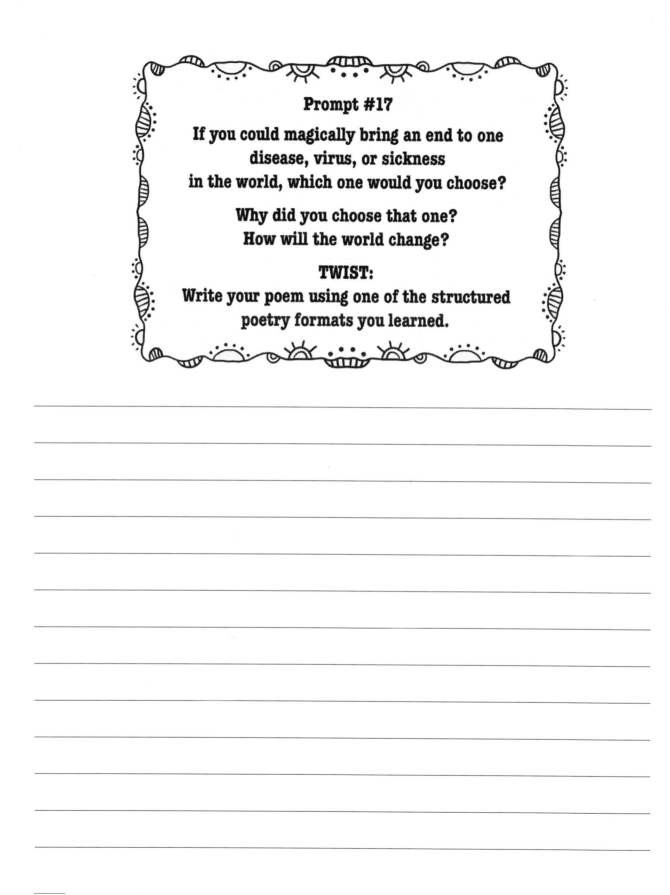

Prompt #17

If you could magically bring an end to one
disease, virus, or sickness
in the world, which one would you choose?

Why did you choose that one?
How will the world change?

TWIST:
Write your poem using one of the structured
poetry formats you learned.

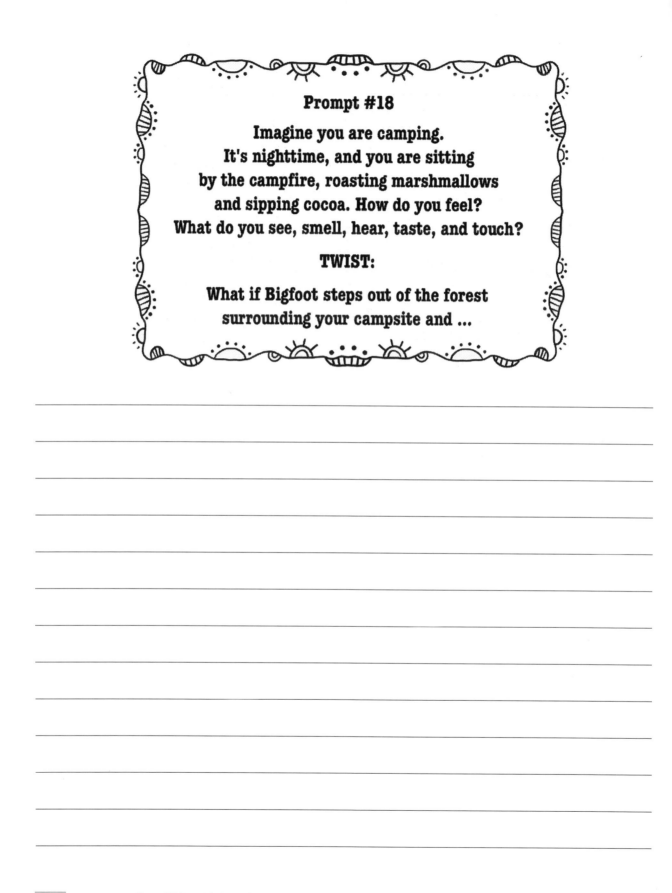

Prompt #18

Imagine you are camping.
It's nighttime, and you are sitting
by the campfire, roasting marshmallows
and sipping cocoa. How do you feel?
What do you see, smell, hear, taste, and touch?

TWIST:

What if Bigfoot steps out of the forest
surrounding your campsite and ...

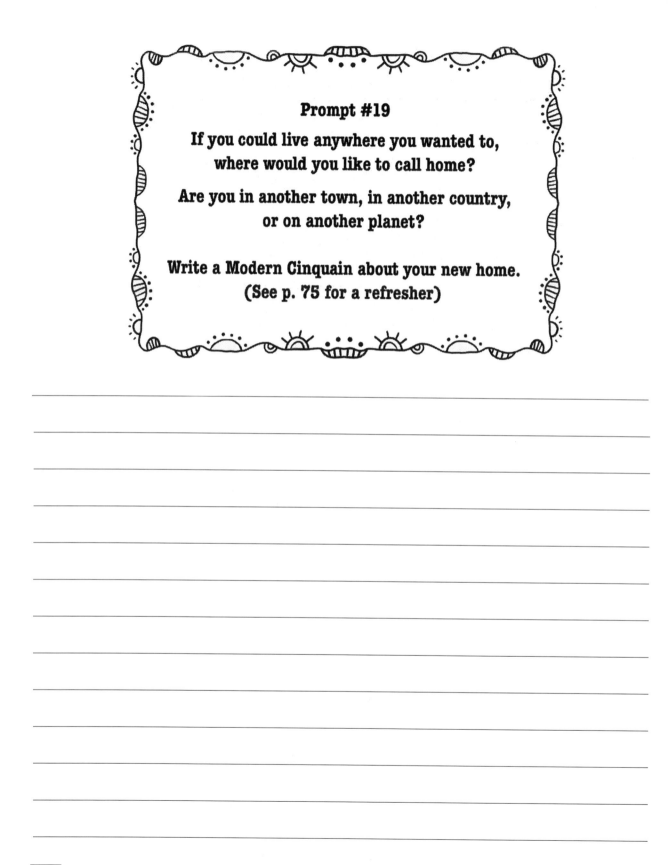

Prompt #19

If you could live anywhere you wanted to,
where would you like to call home?

Are you in another town, in another country,
or on another planet?

Write a Modern Cinquain about your new home.
(See p. 75 for a refresher)

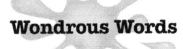

Wondrous Words

INSTEAD OF SAYING "VERY"

Very Stinky:
Putrid, Rank, Pungent

Very Dry:
Parched, Shriveled, Withered

Very Happy:
Elated, Ecstatic, Enchanted

Very Strong:
Capable, Tough, Unyielding

Very Bad:
Atrocious, Lousy, Dreadful

Very Good:
Superb, Exceptional, Satisfying

Very Smart:
Intelligent, Brilliant, Inventive

Very Colorful:
Vibrant, Vivid, Gaudy

Very Neat:
Immaculate, Spotless, Impeccable

Very Tasty:
Delicious, Delectable, Palatable

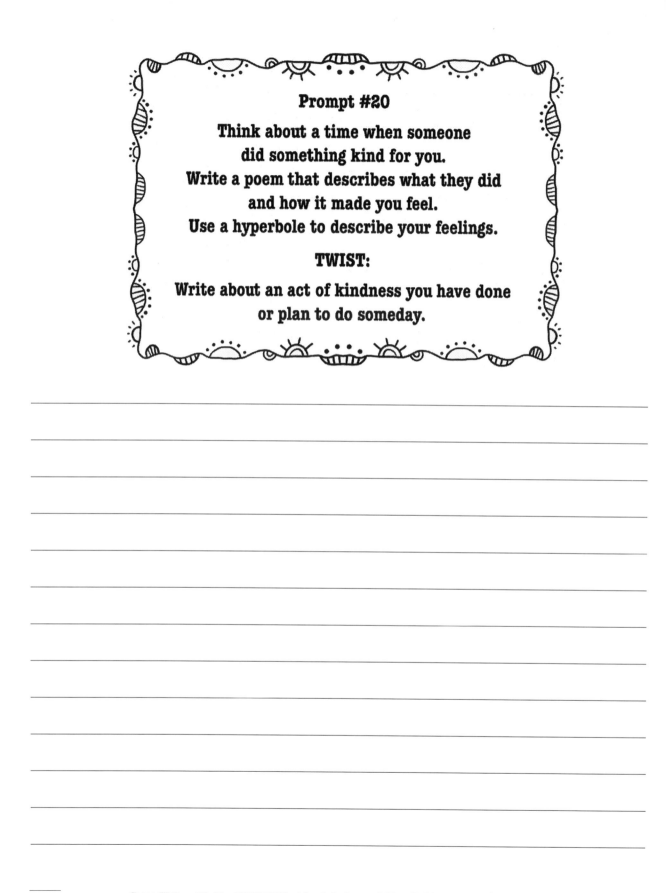

Prompt #20

Think about a time when someone
did something kind for you.
Write a poem that describes what they did
and how it made you feel.
Use a hyperbole to describe your feelings.

TWIST:

Write about an act of kindness you have done
or plan to do someday.

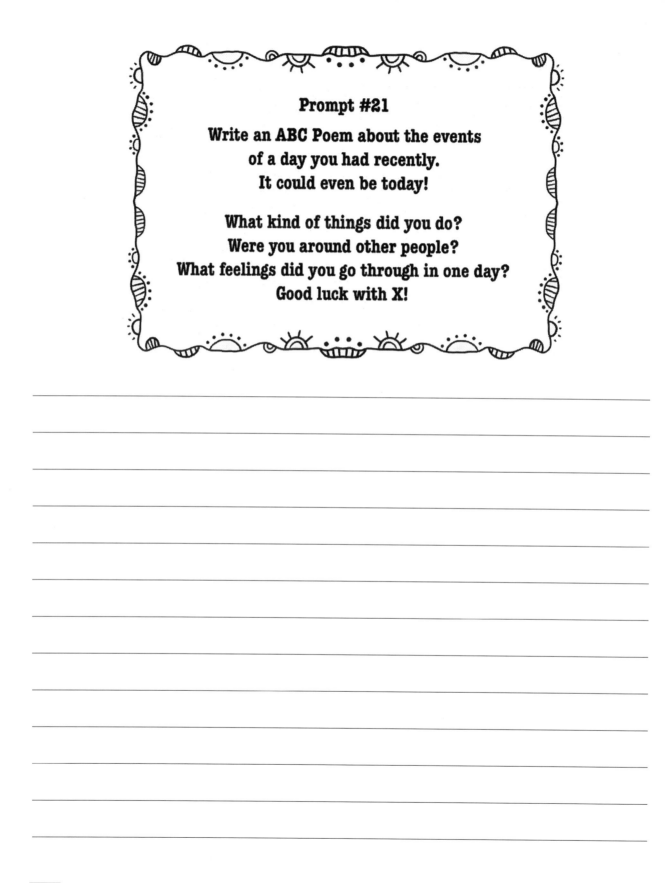

Prompt #21

Write an ABC Poem about the events
of a day you had recently.
It could even be today!

What kind of things did you do?
Were you around other people?
What feelings did you go through in one day?
Good luck with X!

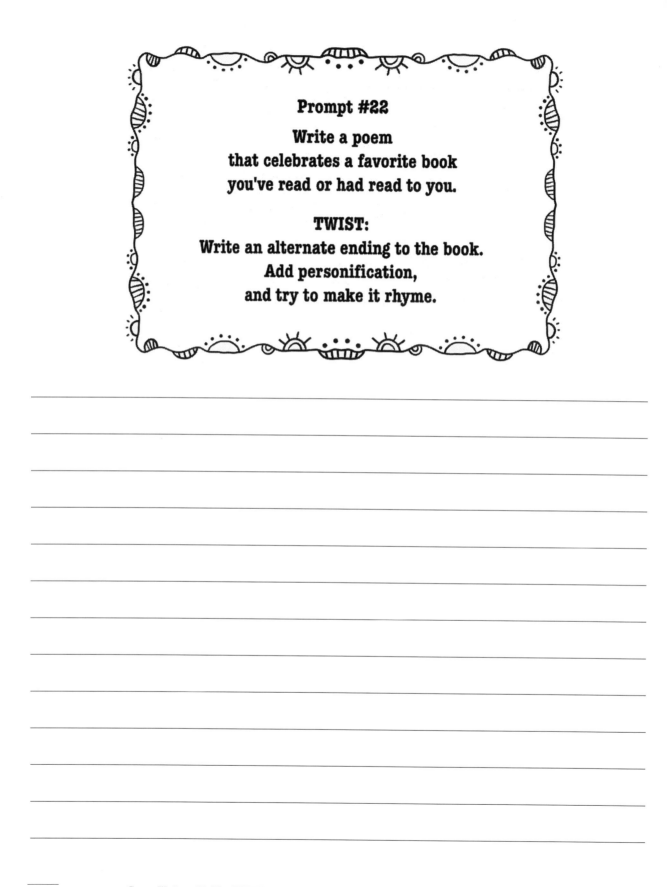

Prompt #22

Write a poem
that celebrates a favorite book
you've read or had read to you.

TWIST:

Write an alternate ending to the book.
Add personification,
and try to make it rhyme.

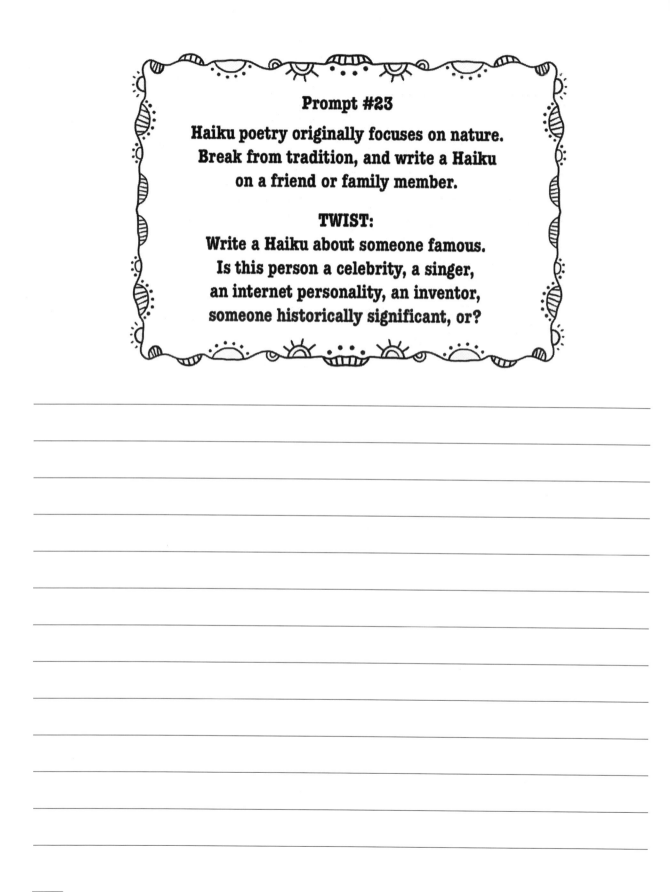

Prompt #23

Haiku poetry originally focuses on nature.
Break from tradition, and write a Haiku
on a friend or family member.

TWIST:

Write a Haiku about someone famous.
Is this person a celebrity, a singer,
an internet personality, an inventor,
someone historically significant, or?

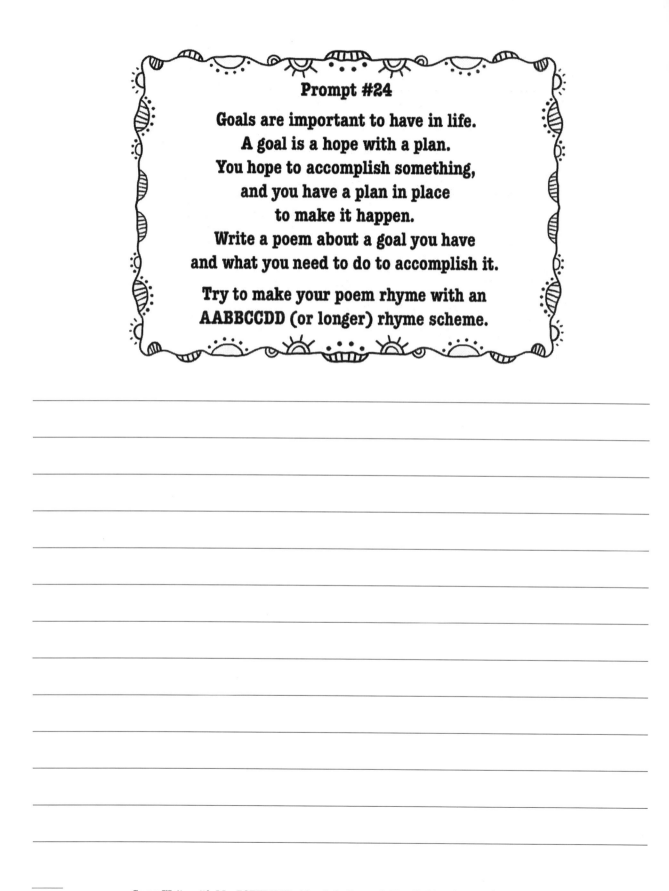

Prompt #24

Goals are important to have in life.
A goal is a hope with a plan.
You hope to accomplish something,
and you have a plan in place
to make it happen.
Write a poem about a goal you have
and what you need to do to accomplish it.

Try to make your poem rhyme with an
AABBCCDD (or longer) rhyme scheme.

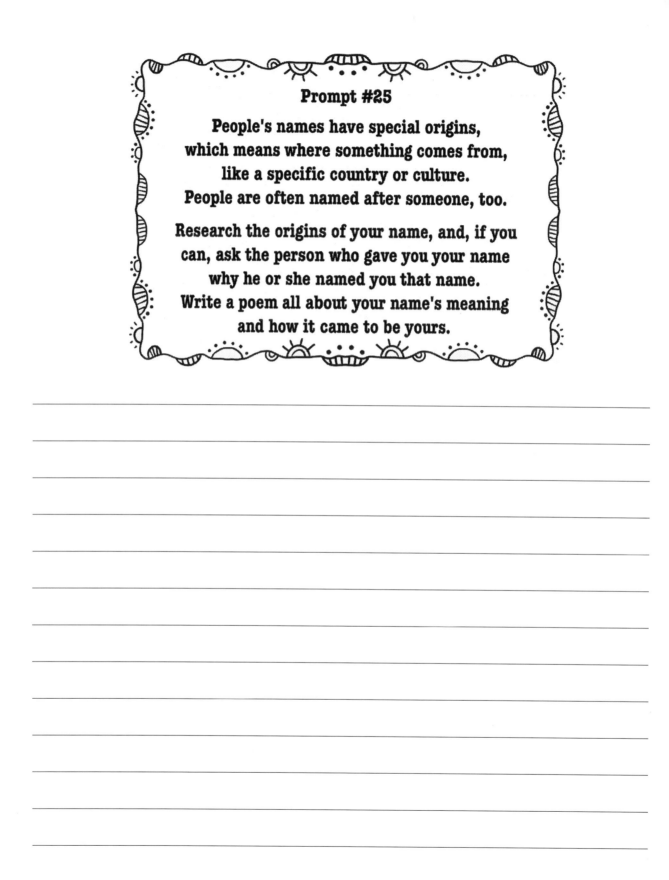

Prompt #25

People's names have special origins,
which means where something comes from,
like a specific country or culture.
People are often named after someone, too.

Research the origins of your name, and, if you
can, ask the person who gave you your name
why he or she named you that name.
Write a poem all about your name's meaning
and how it came to be yours.

Pictorial Inspiration

Hey? Psst! I want to let you know,
before you begin the final exercise,
I've enjoyed every step
of this journey with you.
I am proud to have been cheering you on
as you have developed into a great poet.
Always remember,
you can find inspiration
anywhere you go.
Take in your surroundings
with all of your senses.
Find inspiration in how things
make you feel emotionally.
Let the beauty in this word
move you to find your own voice.
Then write it all down creatively.
In the next section,
you'll see several pictures
meant to inspire your imagination.
When you write a poem for each image,
pack it full of all the skills you've learned.
You can write poems using
a structured format, free verse style,
or you can even play around
with a rhyme scheme of your choice.
Be sure to add poetic devices,
as well as some wondrous words
you've learned along the way.

Until we write together again ...

PICTURE PROMPTS

Dear Writer,

There's an old expression that goes, "A picture is worth a thousand words." That means a picture can inspire many thoughts and feelings which, if written down, would amount to a lot of words. I think simple poems will do for this fun writing exercise!

~Brooke E. Wayne

DIRECTIONS:

First, fill in the brainstorming bubble with words or phrases that come to your mind when you look at the picture. Then use some of those words to write a poem about what you think is happening in the picture. Add a poetic device, like a simile or some alliteration, to your poem. Include how the picture makes you feel or how the people (or creatures) in the picture might be feeling. This style of poem is just a suggestion, though. You can write your poems any way you want to!

thrilling   winners

prize   strong   sweaty

recess   competition

triangle grips were like
helping hands

THE OBSTACLE COURSE
The recess bell rings, the classroom clears, we all meet on the playground.
Sweaty faces taking sides--it's us against them!
Beat the obstacle course with the best time--it's such a thrilling competition!
Tiny triangle grips are like helping hands, swinging us towards the prize.
Winners get to go to lunch first, but everyone wears a winning smile.
We beat them by seconds, swinging swiftly through the air!

PROMPT #1

_____

_____

_____

_____

_____

_____

_____

_____

_____

_____

_____

_____

_____

_____

_____

_____

_____

_____

PROMPT #2

_____

_____

_____

_____

_____

_____

_____

_____

_____

_____

_____

_____

_____

_____

_____

_____

_____

_____

_____

_____

PROMPT #3

PROMPT #4

12

PROMPT #5

_____

_____

_____

_____

_____

_____

_____

_____

_____

_____

_____

_____

_____

_____

_____

_____

_____

_____

_____

PROMPT #6

_____

_____

_____

_____

_____

_____

_____

_____

_____

_____

_____

_____

_____

_____

_____

_____

_____

_____

_____

PROMPT #7

Write

_____

_____

_____

_____

_____

_____

_____

_____

_____

_____

_____

_____

_____

_____

_____

_____

_____

_____

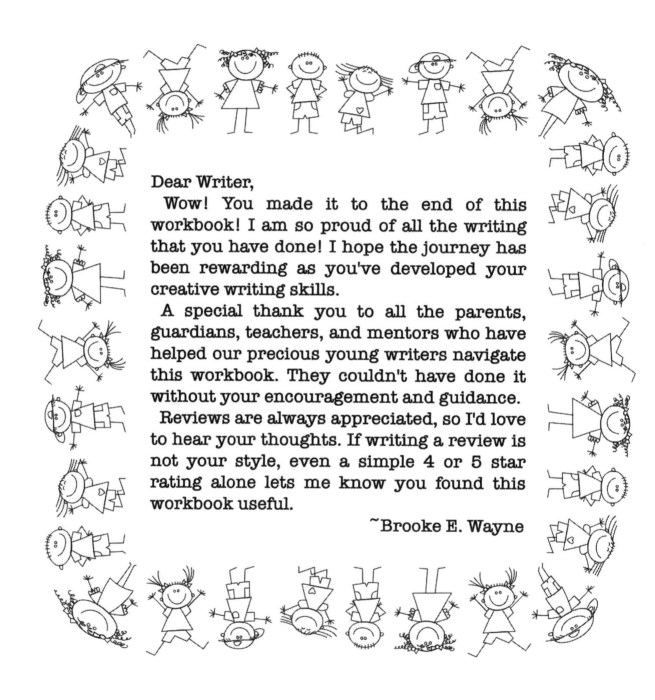

Dear Writer,

Wow! You made it to the end of this workbook! I am so proud of all the writing that you have done! I hope the journey has been rewarding as you've developed your creative writing skills.

A special thank you to all the parents, guardians, teachers, and mentors who have helped our precious young writers navigate this workbook. They couldn't have done it without your encouragement and guidance.

Reviews are always appreciated, so I'd love to hear your thoughts. If writing a review is not your style, even a simple 4 or 5 star rating alone lets me know you found this workbook useful.

~Brooke E. Wayne

How to Write a Review:

Sign into your Amazon Account:

Go to Orders, and Click on "Write a Product Review" on the right side.

You can give a book stars with or without a review.

A review can be as simple as, "I like it because ... I recommend it to ...".

BROOKE E. WAYNE is a Romantic Comedy author who lives the RomCom dream in California. She is married to South Philly born, Eagles-obsessed YouTube Content Creator @philly.500, who she met online and fell in love with long before that kind of meet cute was cool. They have two young daughters who flood their happily-ever-after lives with girly giggles and immeasurable love.

She holds a BA in English with a minor in Theology, a MA in Humanities with an emphasis in Literature, two Clear CLAD credentials, and an unofficial PhD in the Art of Snark.

Never without a journal on hand, Brooke has been writing stories and poetry since she was eleven years old. She's had everything from poetry to articles for an Encyclopedia set published over the last thirty years. Her romance novels and creative writing workbooks are available on Amazon.

When Brooke is not crafting sensual, contemporary romances with light-hearted, witty twists or creative writing workbooks, she teaches English Language Arts, inspiring others to read classic literature and write from the heart.

Brooke E. Wayne

Romance with a Kiss of Humor

www.brookeewayne.com

Made in the USA
Las Vegas, NV
01 August 2023

75488009R00092